Memories From Home

Memories From Home

✦

Cooking with Family & Friends

Linda Weiss

iUniverse, Inc.
New York Lincoln Shanghai

Memories From Home
Cooking with Family & Friends

iUniverse books may be ordered through booksellers or by contacting:

iUniverse
2021 Pine Lake Road, Suite 100
Lincoln, NE 68512
www.iuniverse.com
1-800-Authors (1-800-288-4677)

The views expressed in this work are solely those of the author and do not necessarily reflect the views of the publisher, and the publisher hereby disclaims any responsibility for them.

The author is not responsible for recipes that have errors.

Cover Photo-Luncheon On A Porch © Joshua Ets-Hokin/Corbis

ISBN: 978-0-595-42739-0 (pbk)
ISBN: 978-0-595-87070-7 (ebk)

Printed in the United States of America

Dedicated to My Children
With The Greatest Love

Contents

Writing This Cookbook

This is my first cookbook. I'd like to thank my children, Rob and Ed for all the encouragement they've given when I was ready to give up! And, thank you to my grandchildren, Emily and Rebecca for helping me recipe test.

The book title, Memories From Home is the result of something my dad said to me when an article that I had written about my grandmother appeared on an entire page in my hometown paper. He said tearfully, "you sure brought back a lot of good memories for me." And, I knew that was it, it had to be Memories From Home! Thanks Daddy! I love you.

Since I have been writing for some years now I've included stories about my childhood and stories of growing up in a place that I love the most, the south! There is no place like it on earth. And, if you were lucky enough to be born here, or live here now, you will understand what I mean! It is a world of gracious living, and wonderful kind people.

I couldn't have written this book without the help of all the good cooks in my family who gave me a base to work with, even before I went to Le Cordon Bleu of Paris. I have said this many times, if you don't know what good food taste like, you don't know how to make food taste good! Thanks to my late mother, and my two grandmother's for their wonderful taste in food.

As a personal chef and cooking teacher, I've had the opportunity to find recipes from many different sources and I have shared them with you in this book. Some are recipes that I've developed while others are recipes that my late mother gave me, or that I found hand-written in her recipe booklet after she died. Others are from my grandmothers, my stepmother Janice Rogers, my daddy's sister Aunt Elizabeth, cousins and friends, such as my friend Ellen Thompson who has shared some of her families' best recipes with me. I can tell you that the recipes are all good or they wouldn't be in the book! So, I hope that you will enjoy them.

Thanks to my husband Steve for helping me design the book and put it together. As you can see, I couldn't have done it without him either!

Thanks a million to, Kay McKee, Sara Epperson, Lillian Hart, Marion Lawson, and Edith Triguero, also known as "the front table" at almost every cooking class I've taught. They are more than my friends! They are a huge part of my life! And, thanks to all my friends who have attended my classes over the years.

Thanks to Joyce McCarrell, Wendy Walls, Florence Cashion, and Cici Goodyear at Williams Sonoma. Couldn't have done any of this without you!

Thanks to my good friends Judy Booker and Brenda Thompson at Judy Booker's Kitchen Emporium. And, to Gay and Mack McLeskey at the new Kitchen Emporium. How can I ever thank you for all you have done my friends!

Thanks also to the editors who believed in me enough to give me the opportunity to write for their magazines. I will forever appreciate all you have done to foster my writing spirit.

And, thanks to Heather Sullivan, the morning anchor at CBS, channel 7 in Greenville, Spartanburg. It was great working with you my friend. Thank you for having me on the air so often. And, to Peggy Denny, and her television crew at channel 16, Dove Broadcasting for all you've done. I always enjoy being there. And, thank you so very much.

Becoming a Personal Chef

In 1997, after attending Le Cordon Bleu of Paris, I decided to become a personal chef. My first clients were my neighbors whose daughter had just married in North Carolina. My neighbors flew their family and friends from San Marino, Italy to Chapel Hill, NC for the wedding and then flew them back to their home in Florida for a farewell party before flying them back home to Italy. Fortunately, they were also my friends and lived right around the corner from me and when it was time for the party, I was invited to cook for them.

We settled on a menu of Salmon Niçoise Salad for the main dish. A few days before the party I was told by the hostess that she was extremely nervous because her husband didn't like salmon and she was afraid that he would be upset, but she wanted to keep the menu as it was. I served the dish, and held my breath. Shortly after dinner, I heard heavy footsteps coming toward the kitchen from the dining room. It was the host. He came directly toward me, and gave me the biggest kiss! He not only loved the salmon but the entire dinner. Needless to say, I was very happy and very relieved, and his wife was a heroine for choosing such a great menu for his family from Italy!

Word got around about the salmon, and I was called by a high-profile person in town to prepare the salmon dish for a group of 100 people. They loved it, and many people came into the kitchen to see how I had prepared it and to get the recipe. I was still preparing food for their parties when we moved to South Carolina and I became the personal chef for other high profile clients, as well as people who have become my dear friends.

While I was in Florida, I signed up for temporary jobs with some of the largest restaurants on theme park property. I thought it would be a great opportunity to work in some of the larger, more organized restaurants to find out how food was made in large quantities, but mainly how it was stored. This was a gray area for me. Working on temporary jobs is another story, but if you want to know the real truth, just ask me the next time we meet!

Being a personal chef is fun and exciting. I have liked everyone that I've had the opportunity to work with. And, I have always learned something and grown in some way. Unfortunately, when I became a Personal Chef, I couldn't find much written information about food storage, so I have decided that I will give you some suggestions to make it easier for you to store, and reheat the food that you make in advance, whether for yourself or others.

These days I teach cooking classes and write articles about food, as well as doing television shows. But, I loved working as a Personal Chef. It's a great job! See the end of the book for storage tips.

Beverages

Champagne Punch

This punch reminds me of the first time I crashed a party. My grandmother had been invited to a wedding tea at Miss Lovie Downey's home next door. I was very young at the time, and "Mommy" left me with her cook and went to the tea. I slipped away, and went through the back door of the home where the tea was being held. My grandmother was very upset with me and tried to take me home, but everyone wanted me to stay and enjoy the party too, so I did. I remember that day so well. The punch was beautiful and very tasty. That was also the day that I started my love affair with petite fours, and little tiny tea sandwiches.

1 (12-ounce) can frozen orange juice concentrate, thawed
1 (12-ounce) can frozen lemonade concentrate, thawed
1 quart apple or pineapple juice
6 cups water
2 bottles chilled Dry Champagne

Combine all the ingredients except the Champagne. Chill for 4-6 hours. When ready to serve, add the Champagne. Pour the punch into a large punch bowl. Make 5 quarts.
NOTE: You can always use sparkling white grape juice as a substitute for the Champagne. Sparkling white grape juice is actually a little sweeter.

Tea Time Banana Punch

My friend Ellen gave me this recipe. I served it at an "Afternoon Tea" cooking class and it was a great success.

3 ½ cups sugar
6 cups water
3 cups pineapple juice
2 cups orange juice
2 lemons, juiced
3 large or 4 small bananas mashed
1 (2 liter) bottle ginger ale or 7-Up

Place sugar and water in a saucepan. Heat to a boil and stir until sugar is dissolved. Cool. Add other ingredients except ginger ale. Freeze for 24 hours in a 6 quart container with a lid. Remove from the freezer and thaw to a slush about 2-3 hours before serving time. Mash out any lumps with a potato masher. Add the ginger ale when ready to serve. It should be slushy. You can make a ring of frozen punch, add strawberries or cherries for decoration before freezing, or float them in the punch. Serves 30.

Sparkling Fruit

We were doing a photo shoot for a magazine and I wanted to use something with color for the background. I used sparkling white grape juice to simulate wine, poured it in glasses and then filled the glasses with fruit. After the shoot, the editor and I drank the "fruit" for lunch and I realized that it was so good that I'd have to make it again, and again.

1 bottle Sparking Grape Juice (Catawba if you can find it)
1 large container mixed fruit, such as grapes, cantaloupe,
Honeydew, strawberries, pineapple

Place desired amount of fruit in glasses and pour sparkling white grape juice over the fruit. Serve chilled.

Sweet Mint Julep

2/3 cup bourbon
1 tablespoon water
1-1/2 tablespoons confectioner's sugar
8-9 sprigs fresh mint
Shaved ice

Combine all ingredients and serve over shaved ice in a julep cup. Serves 2.

Southern Iced Tea

2-1/4 cups sugar
8 regular size tea bags
2 cups orange juice
1 cup lemon juice

Combine 2 cups water and sugar, boil for 5 minutes. Steep the tea bags in 1 quart of boiling water for 5 minutes. Put into two quarts of cold water. Add remaining ingredients. Serves 12-20.
Note: The easiest way that I have found to steep the bags is to put them in a glass container (must be heat resistant) and cover the top with a plate or saucer, depending on the size. The dish keeps the water from evaporating, and keeps the water hotter. This is the way that Sara always made our tea.

Hot Toddy Holiday Punch

3 cups unsweetened pineapple juice
3 cups cranberry-apple juice drink
1 cup water
1/3 cup firmly packed light brown sugar
2 lemon slices
2 (4") cinnamon sticks, broken
1-½ teaspoons whole cloves
Cinnamon sticks (optional)

Pour juices into a 12-cup percolator. Place brown sugar and next 3 ingredients in percolator basket. Perk through completer cycle of electric percolator. Serve with cinnamon sticks, if desired. Yield: 7 cups.

Appetizers

Sinful Apricot Brie

12 sheets phyllo dough
2-3 sticks butter, melted
1 (5-pound) whole brie, not fully ripe
1 (12-ounce) jar apricot preserves

Preheat the oven to 350º. Butter a 13 X 9-inch baking sheet.
Layer 6 sheets of phyllo on the baking sheet, staggering the layers to create a circle, brushing each layer with melted butter. Place brie in center of phyllo and spread top and sides with apricot preserves. Fold the phyllo up around the cheese. Cover the top of the cheese with 6 sheets of phyllo, again staggering layers and brushing each with butter. Smooth top and sides. Tuck ends under Brie. Brush top and sides with butter. Bake at 350º for 20-30 minutes or until golden brown.
Let stand for 30-45 minutes before serving. Cut into small wedges.
Note: Use the same procedure for smaller brie, but use a smaller amount of preserves. Use any preserves that you like.

Baked Artichoke Florentine Spread

2 (10-ounce) packages frozen chopped spinach, thawed
2 (7-ounce) jars marinated artichokes, drained and chopped
1-1/2 (8-ounce) packages cream cheese, softened
1 cup freshly grated Parmesan cheese
½ cup mayonnaise
3 large garlic cloves, minced
2 tablespoons fresh lemon juice
1-1/2 cups French bread crumbs
2 tablespoons butter, melted

Drain spinach by squeezing in your hands or between paper towels until all excess moisture is removed. Combine the artichokes, spinach and the next 5 ingredients in a large bowl. Mix well. Pour into a greased baking dish or a soufflé dish. Melt butter and mix with the bread crumbs. Sprinkle over the baking dish. Bake uncovered at 375º for 25 minutes, or until bubbly. Serve with toasted baguettes. Note: The spread can be made a day ahead and refrigerated. Add another 10-15 minutes to the cooking time.

Toasted Baguettes

2 pre-sliced French baguettes
Butter or olive oil
Garlic powder

Spread slices with butter or olive oil. Sprinkle with garlic powder. Place on a baking sheet and put them into a 375º oven until toasted.
*Storage tip: Place the butter or olive oil on the baguette slices and sprinkle with garlic powder. Place slices in a plastic bag and store in the refrigerator until ready to toast.

South Carolina Crab Dip

1 pound fresh crab meat, drained and flaked
3 (8-ounce) packages cream cheese, softened
2-4 tablespoons milk
½ cup chopped green onions
3-5 tablespoons horseradish cream sauce

Combine all ingredients in the bowl of an electric mixer. Mix until well blended. Place the crab mixture in a baking dish and bake in a preheated 350º oven until bubbly and the top is lightly browned. Serve with crackers.

Cheese Marinade

Mother gave me this recipe. I have used it for many years at holiday parties. It's always a big hit. If you serve this at a party, you will be asked for the recipe.

½ cup vegetable oil
½ cup white wine vinegar
1 small jar diced pimientos, drained
3 tablespoons chopped fresh parsley
3 tablespoons thinly slice green onions
3 cloves garlic, minced
1 teaspoon sugar
1 teaspoon dried basil
½ teaspoon salt
½ teaspoon pepper
1 (8-ounce) package cream cheese, chilled
1 (8-ounce) block sharp cheddar cheese, chilled (same size package as cream cheese)
Fresh parsley sprigs

Combine the first 10 ingredients in a jar. Cover tightly, and shake rattle and roll! Set aside. Cut the block of cheddar in half lengthwise and then cut ¼-inch slices crosswise. Repeat the procedure with the cream cheese. In a shallow glass dish, arrange the cheese squares, alternating a Cheddar slice and a cream cheese slice, until all slices have been used. You may want to make two logs. Pour the marinade over the cheese slices. Refrigerate for 8 hours or overnight. Transfer the cheese slices to a serving platter in the same way that you have placed them in the bowl. Spoon the marinade over the slices and sprinkle with parsley. Serves 16.
Note: I use really good assorted crisp crackers with this dish. I also serve the cheese in a long shallow crystal dish set inside a rectangular silver tray and I put the crackers around the edge of the silver tray.

Chevŕe Wrapped in Vine Leaves

1 jar grape leaves
1 (10-ounce) log goat cheese
Balsamic vinegar
1 garlic clove, minced
1 tablespoon Greek oregano

Remove enough grape leaves from the brine to wrap around ¾-inch slices of goat cheese from the log. Rinse the grape leaves to remove the brine, and marinate in balsamic vinegar in the refrigerator for 2-3 days. Remove the leaves from the vinegar and dry them. Wrap a slice of goat cheese in a leaf. Mix the olive oil, garlic and oregano. Dip the leaves with goat cheese into this mixture. Grill for 1-1/2 minutes on each side, or bake for 10 minutes in a preheated 375º oven. Serve on toasted baguette slices.

Dates Stuffed with Goat Cheese wrapped in Bacon

I really enjoy this recipe. It could be used for dessert if you substitute the goat cheese for mascarpone, add toasted chopped nuts and leave out the bacon. This recipe has been around for ages on appetizer menus.

1 pound dates, seeded
4 ounces goat cheese, slightly softened
Thinly sliced bacon or proscuitto

Preheat oven to 350º. Place the goat cheese in a pastry bag. Pipe the goat cheese into the hollowed date. Wrap the date, one wrap around with thinly sliced bacon. Secure with a toothpick if necessary. Place in an oiled, ovenproof baking dish. Bake for 15-20 minutes or until bacon is crisp. Serve hot or at room temperature.

Goat Cheese and Sun-dried Tomatoes with Basil

1 (11-ounce) log goat cheese
½ cup sun-dried tomatoes in olive oil, drained
¼ cup loosely packed basil leaves
1 tablespoons olive oil

Place the goat cheese log on a serving platter. Chop the drained sun-dried tomatoes, and place in a small bowl. Slice the basil into thin slices, and add to the tomatoes. Add the olive oil. Spoon the tomato basil mixture on top of the goat cheese. Serve with good crackers or baguettes.

Little Charleston Benne Seed Wafers

2 cups flour
1 teaspoon salt
Dash of cayenne pepper
Sea salt or kosher salt
¾ cups shortening
Ice water (4 tablespoons) as needed
1 cup roasted sesame seeds

Cook sesame seeds in a heavy skillet over medium heat for 5 minutes or until toasted. Set aside to cool. Mix dry ingredients: cut in shortening; add ice water to make dough the consistency of a piecrust. Add the sesame seeds. Roll thin and cut into 1-inch round wafers. Place on a sheet pan and cook in a 300° oven for 20-25 minutes or until light brown and crisp. Sprinkle with sea or kosher salt as soon as removed from the oven. Keep in a covered tin or jar. Put back in the oven to crisp before serving. Makes several dozen.

Mae's Peppery Cheese Wafers

Mae is Judy Booker's mother-in-law. And, she is my friend and a great cook. Mae makes these little wafers in miniature Madeleine molds. Wish I had thought of that!

1 cup softened butter
4 cups shredded sharp Cheddar cheese
2 cups all-purpose flour
2 cups finely chopped pecans
1 teaspoon cayenne pepper
1-1/2 teaspoons salt

Cream butter and cheese together. Add other ingredients and mix well. Roll into a log (or logs) and refrigerate for several hours. Slice into thin rounds. Place on lightly greased cookie sheets and bake at 350º for 20 minutes or until edges are slightly browned. Or slice and press into mini Madeleine molds.

Mrs. Taylor's Honeysuckle Vine Crackers & Preserves

One of my favorite snacks as a child was a jar of fig preserves and a box of saltines that my sister Margaret, and friends, Pat and Bammy ate under a honeysuckle vine "cave" in Miss Mary Lou Taylor's yard. They were the best but these are even better. Great when you just want a little something for dessert too!

1 (7-ounce) box buttery crackers (I used DARE Cabaret Crackers)
1 jar of your favorite fig preserves
1 (8-ounce) container mascarpone cheese or goat cheese-optional

Spread the crackers with the fig preserves or top with mascarpone and then put the preserves on top. You can't get any better in life than this!

Cheese Ring & Strawberry Preserves

The original recipe for the Cheese Ring is from The Carter Family Cookbook, and it calls for the cheese to be mashed against the side of the bowl. In the "old days" cheese was sold on a hoop, or round. And, it was not refrigerated, so it would have had a softer texture. Daddy would send Gray Dial down to Campbell, on the Tombigbee River to get "hoop cheese." I remember my father taking the cheese out of the cabinet where it was stored in white waxy paper. He would get a knife and cut off slices to eat with crackers and savor it with a little "toddy" about 5PM every day.

1 pound grated sharp cheddar
1-1/2 cups pecans chopped and toasted (see note)
¼ small sweet onion, cut into chunks
2 tablespoons milk
¼ teaspoon black pepper
Dash of cayenne pepper
½ cup mayonnaise or more to bind the ingredients
Good strawberry preserves

Place the cheese, onion, milk and mayonnaise in a food processor fitted with a steel blade. Pulse until well mixed. Add more mayonnaise if needed. Remove from processor and add pecans. Spoon into a bowl that has been lined with plastic wrap, Cover and refrigerate. When ready to serve, unmold onto a serving plate or cake pedestal. Make an indention or hole in the center of the cheese and add the strawberry preserves. Serve with buttery crackers.
*"Toast" the pecans on a plate in the microwave for 2 minutes on high. Watch to make sure they don't burn. Cool before adding to the cheese mixture. Every microwave has different levels of power, so it may take more or less time for different microwaves.

Cheese Squares Florentine

Great party food!

1 cup all-purpose flour
1 teaspoon salt
1 teaspoon baking powder
2 eggs, slightly beaten
1 cup milk
3 tablespoons butter, melted
1 pound sharp cheddar cheese, shredded or grated
½ cup onion, finely minced
10 ounce frozen chopped spinach, thawed and drained

Preheat oven to 325º Grease a 9 x 13-inch baking dish. Mix flour, salt, baking powder in a large bowl. Add eggs, milk, butter, cheese and onion. Squeeze spinach to remove excess moisture. Add spinach to cheese mixture and mix well. Spread mixture evenly in the baking dish. Bake for 30-45 minutes. Cool slightly and then cut into small squares. Serves 25.

Green Chili, Cheese & Bacon Dip

2 (8-ounce) packages cream cheese
½ cup mayonnaise
1 tablespoon lemon juice
1 (4-ounce) can chopped green chilies
1 cup minced onion
½ cup green pepper, finely chopped
10 slices crispy fried bacon, drained and crumbled
1 clove garlic, finely chopped
1 large red bell pepper
Corn chips

Combine the cream cheese, mayonnaise and lemon juice in a food processor. Process until smooth. Combine the cream cheese mixture, chilies, onion, pepper, bacon and garlic in a bowl. And mix well. Chill for several hours.
Cut a slice from the top of the red bell pepper and discard. Remove the seed and membrane. Spoon the cream cheese mixture into the red pepper. Serve with corn chips. 2 Cups.

Cucumber Sandwiches

Great for tea time!

English hot house cucumbers
1 loaf Pepperidge Farm thin sliced sandwich bread
Whipped cream cheese
Dilly seasoning by McCormick (in the spice section) (this appears to be a mixture of lemon and dill)

Peel and thinly slice English hot house cucumbers. Spread two slices of bread with whipped cream cheese and sprinkle lightly with the "Dilly" seasoning. Place the cucumber slices on the bread. Use cutters to cut inside the crust for small sandwiches. Or cut the crust off and slice in half crosswise for a triangle. The sandwiches can be refrigerated by placing a damp paper towel between layers and covering tightly.

Curry, Almond Cheese

I made this cheese spread recipe for Mrs. Rose when I was her personal chef. She enjoyed it in the evening with some good crackers and a glass of wine.

2 (8-ounce) packages cream cheese
1 (9-ounce) jar mango chutney
1 cup slivered or sliced almonds, toasted
1 tablespoon curry powder (or to taste)

Process the ingredients in a food processor until slightly smooth, scraping down the sides of the processor once. Mound or mold onto a plate. Cover and chill until ready to serve. Serve with good crackers.

Stuffed Eggs

My son Ed says that I make the best stuffed eggs he's ever had. This is the recipe I use. The secret is in the crackers, whether it's saltines or Ritz.

6 hard boiled eggs
2-4 tablespoons pickle relish
4 crumbled Ritz or Townhouse crackers
Enough mayonnaise to moisten well

Cut the eggs in half. Mix the yolk, pickle, crackers and mayonnaise. Stuff the eggs, and sprinkle with paprika. Place the eggs on a bed of pretty lettuce.

Tombigbee River Pimiento & Cheese

My mother, Ann, made pimiento and cheese every Sunday in the summer for our boating picnics on the Tombigbee River. Along with the pimiento and cheese, our picnic basket had pineapple, fried chicken, ham and desserts. We loved those Summer Sundays of skiing and picnicking on the Tombigbee.

1 package pre-shredded sharp cheddar (2 cups)
1 pepper from a jar of "sweet pimiento," flame roasted peppers (available in the pickle section of most grocery stores)
Mayonnaise to moisten well

Place all ingredients in a food processor with a steel blade. Pulse until mixed. You can use any kind of cheese for this, including the Mexican cheese found in the dairy case. This appetizer or spread can be made a day before serving, and will keep for several days refrigerated.

Mini Tomato Pies for a Tea Party

Mini phyllo tart shells (find these in the frozen food section)
Roma tomatoes—sliced ¼-inch thick
Pimiento & cheese

Make the pimiento and cheese according to the recipe in the index. Place the tart shells on a baking sheet. Fill the tart shells with a small amount of pimiento and cheese. Top each tart with a Roma tomato slice. Bake in a preheated 300° oven until cheese is melted and the tart is bubbly.

Mushroom Pâté

When I'm ready to serve this pâté, I unmold it onto a cake pedestal. Then I put a rosemary sprig on top and surround the pâté with Rosemary Crackers found in the "good" cracker section of the grocery store.

1 pound fresh mushrooms, chopped
3 tablespoons butter
1 (8-ounce) package 1/3 less-fat cream cheese
1 teaspoon lemon pepper
½ teaspoon garlic salt
Fresh rosemary Sprigs

Melt butter in a large skillet over medium-high heat. Add chopped mushrooms. Cook mushrooms about 15-20 minutes or until very tender and all liquid has evaporated. Set aside to cool. When mushrooms are cool, place in a food processor fitted with the steel blade; add the cream cheese, lemon pepper and garlic powder. Process until completely smooth, stopping once to scrape down the sides of the processor. Pour the pâté into a greased mold or a plastic wrap lined bowl or mold. Cover and chill for several hours or overnight. Unmold, and place a rosemary sprig on top. The pâté can be made a day ahead and kept refrigerated until ready to serve.
*I have seen the pate served with green, pimiento stuffed olives, sliced thin and spiraled around the sides like a pineapple. If you have time and patience to place them this would make a beautiful presentation.

Texas Okra Ham Rolls

½ pound thinly sliced red pepper ham
1 (8-ounce) container cream cheese with chives—whipped if available
1 jar pickled okra—from Texas!

Lay the ham pieces on a flat surface. Spread with cream cheese. Trim the ends of the okra. Lay the okra end to end on the ham slice. Roll up tightly. Chill. Slice into 1-inch pieces to serve. Serve on a bed of watercress or red leaf lettuce.

Ham Salad

Mother always served ham salad during the holidays. But, it's good anytime served on a cracker or on a cocktail biscuit such as a tiny angel biscuit. The angel biscuit recipe is in the bread section. To serve the ham on angel biscuits, cut the biscuits very small. Also makes a good sandwich!

2 cups baked ham
½ cup chopped green onions
½ cup finely chopped bell pepper
½ cup finely chopped celery
Finely diced pickles (optional)
Mayonnaise
1 teaspoon Dijon mustard (optional)
Salt and pepper to taste

Place ham in a food processor and pulse until finely chopped. Remove to a bowl. Add green onions, bell pepper, and celery. Add pickle if you like. Add enough mayonnaise (and Dijon mustard) to moisten well.

Ham "Biscuits"

I just love this little recipe for cocktails. In fact, I sent it to a Michigan friend that I met at The Greenbrier. She was a caterer in Grosse Point. She sent me a note telling me that she had used this dish for a picnic and everyone loved it! It is not my original recipe in case you have not seen it before. It's been around for a long time here in the Carolinas.

1 cup butter, softened
3 tablespoons poppy seeds
1 small onion, minced
3 tablespoons yellow mustard
1 teaspoon Worcestershire sauce
3 packages Pepperidge Farm party rolls split
1 pound of boiled ham or Black Forest ham
¾ pound Swiss cheese, sliced

Cream the butter with the mustard, poppy seed, grated onion and Worcestershire sauce. Spread both sides of the rolls with the butter mixture. Divide the ham and cheese evenly on the rolls. Wrap in foil, and bake at 400º for 10 minutes. Cut into individual rolls. May be frozen before baking.
Note: If you would like to make larger sandwiches, use a hoagie roll. Wrap in foil and bake at 400° until heated through.

Salami Pastry Puffs

6 ounces puff pastry dough, thawed
8 slices Italian salami
¼ cup shredded Cheddar
1 egg to glaze

Preheat the oven to 400º. On a floured surface, roll out the pastry dough to 1/8-inch thickness. With a 4-inch fluted cookie cutter, cut out 8 circles of dough. Lay a salami slice in the center of each dough circle. Put a little cheese on top of the salami slice. Brush around the dough circle with the beaten egg. Fold the dough circle in half, press edges to seal. Brush the top of each puff with beaten egg. Bake for 15 minutes or until well risen and golden brown.

Savory Sausage, Pecan & Date Balls

1 pound pork sausage
2 cups biscuit mix
½ cup finely chopped pecans, toasted
1 (8-ounce) package pitted dates, chopped

Combine all ingredients. Mix well. Roll into small balls the size of a walnut. Place on baking sheets that have been sprayed with a non-stick cooking spray. Bake at 350º for 20 minutes. Serve warm. 4 + dozen. Note: This is a great party food.

Cheese Sausage Rolls

I found this in my recipe collection written on brown paper torn from a bag!

1 (16-ounce) package pork sausage, mild or hot
1 (8-ounce) package cream cheese, softened
2 (8-count) packages refrigerated crescent rolls
½ stick butter, melted
Poppy seeds

Brown sausage in a skillet, stirring to crumble. Drain well. Add cream cheese to sausage and mix until melted. Separate the dough into triangles. Spoon about 3 tablespoons of the sausage mixture into the center of the wide ends of the rolls. Shape into rolls according to package directions. Brush rolls with melted butter and sprinkle with poppy seeds. Place on a baking sheet and bake at 375º for 12-15 minutes.

Aunt Betty's Shrimp Mold

1 (10-ounce) can tomato soup
3 (3-ounce) packages cream cheese at room temperature
1 envelope unflavored gelatin
¼ cup cold water
2 cups boiled peeled shrimp, seasoned and finely chopped*
1 cup mayonnaise
½ cup finely diced celery
¼ cup very finely diced green onion
1 tablespoon lemon juice
Dash of garlic powder
Salt, pepper and red pepper to taste

*Shrimp—this would be shrimp cooked in shrimp boil according to package directions.
Heat the soup and dissolve the cream cheese in it. Soak the gelatin in the cold water and when softened, add to the soup mixture. Let the soup mixture cool to room temperature, about 1-1/2 hours. Add all other ingredients. Pour into an oiled mold and chill overnight. Place on a platter surrounded with crackers.

Mt. Pleasant Pickled Shrimp

2 quarts water
1 pound peeled, deveined shrimp
3 tablespoons Creole seasoning
3 large shallots, thinly sliced
1 small green bell pepper, cut into thin slices
1 small red bell pepper, cut into thin slices
1-1/2 cups water
¾ cups white vinegar
1 tablespoon salt

Bring 8 cups water to a boil in a large pan. Add shrimp and Creole seasoning. Boil for 4 minutes. Place shrimp in a jar or a non-reactive bowl. Add sliced shallots and peppers. Add salt, vinegar, and 1-1/2 cups water. Stir to blend in with shrimp. Cover and chill for several hours before serving. Drain, serve as an appetizer. 8-10 Appetizer servings.

Louisiana Bayou Shrimp

3 quarts water
1 large lemon, sliced
4-1/2 pounds peeled large shrimp
2 cups vegetable oil
3 tablespoons hot sauce
4 large garlic cloves, minced
1 teaspoon salt
1-1/2 teaspoons seafood seasoning
1-1/2 teaspoons dried basil
1-1/2 teaspoons dried oregano
1-1/2 teaspoons dried thyme
2 tablespoon fresh minced parsley

Bring the water and lemon to a boil. Add the shrimp and cook until shrimp are done. This will take about 5 minutes. Drain well. Place the shrimp in a large plastic storage bag and add the remaining ingredients. Seal the bag and let shrimp marinate in the refrigerator for 6-8 hours or overnight. Drain well, and place shrimp on a large serving platter or in a large bowl. Place lemon slices on top and sprinkle with some extra minced parsley. 12-15 Appetizer servings.

Sun-dried Tomato Spread

1 (8-ounce) package cream cheese, softened
3 tablespoons of a 10-ounce jar of Sun-dried tomato pesto

Add the cream cheese and 3 tablespoons of the pesto to mixing bowl or food processor. Mix until thoroughly blended. Serve with toasted baguettes.
See toasted baguettes in recipe section. Sun-dried tomato pesto can usually be found in the pasta section of the grocery store. This appetizer can be made a day in advance and kept refrigerated.

Heavenly Baked Sweet Onion Dip

The first time I had this I couldn't stop eating it. I was eating it with the chip crumbs left at the bottom of the bowl! Great served in a chafing dish.

3 large sweet onions such as Vidalia or Texas Sweet, finely chopped
4 tablespoons unsalted butter
2 cups Swiss or Gruyere cheese
2 cups mayonnaise
1 clove garlic, minced
¼-1/2 teaspoon hot sauce
¼ cup white wine

Sauté the onions in butter until tender. Mix the cheese, mayonnaise, hot sauce, garlic and wine in a large mixing bowl. Add the onions and mix well. Spoon the mixture into a buttered or sprayed casserole dish. Bake in a 375° oven for 20-25 minutes until cheese has melted. Serve with tortilla chips.

Holiday Stuffed Mushrooms

24 medium size Portobello mushrooms, or white mushrooms
2 tablespoons butter
½ pound hot Italian sausage, casing removed
1 clove garlic, finely chopped
¼ teaspoon pepper
Freshly grated Parmesan cheese

Clean the mushrooms. Remove stems and set aside. Melt the butter in a large skillet. Cook mushroom caps in the butter over medium-high heat, stirring constantly about 5 minutes. Drain mushrooms. Place mushroom caps, stems side up on a large rack set on a baking sheet or broiler pan. Set aside.
Combine sausage, and garlic in a large skillet. Cook over medium-high heat until sausage browns and crumbles. Drain well. In a food processor with a steel blade, process sausage, mushroom stems and pepper for about 20 seconds. Spoon mixture into mushroom caps and sprinkle with Parmesan cheese. Broil about 5 inches from heat for 3-4 minutes or until thoroughly heated. Makes 2 dozen mushroom caps.

Pizza Bitty Bites

1 pound pork sausage
1 cup chopped onions
1-1/2 cups shredded sharp cheddar cheese
1/2 cup grated parmesan cheese
1-1/2 teaspoon dried oregano
1 teaspoon garlic salt
1 (8-ounce) can tomato sauce
1 (6-ounce) can tomato paste
2 cans flaky—style biscuits
Shredded mozzarella cheese

Simmer sausage until half done. Add onions, and cook until both are done. Drain. Add sharp Cheddar and parmesan cheese, oregano, garlic salt, tomato paste, and tomato sauce and simmer 20 minutes. Cool. Take 12 biscuits from 1 can and separate each biscuit into 4 layers. Place on a cookie sheet. Add 1 teaspoon of pizza mixture to the top of each layer. Repeat the process on second can of biscuits. Freeze on a cookie sheet. Remove when frozen and place in plastic bags in freezer. When ready to serve, take from the freezer and add mozzarella cheese. Place on a cookie sheet and bake in a 350° oven until the pizzas are bubbly and cooked through. Makes approximately 100.

Salads

Main Dish Salads

Salmon Niçoise is one of my absolute favorite salads. It's not only good, but beautiful. It can be served in the hottest summer or during the holidays for a party. I have been making it for years, long before I went to Le Cordon Bleu. It's a great salad with salmon cooked in a bourbon, soy sauce mixture and cold vegetables with a vinaigrette dressing.

It's easy, it's elegant and your friends, like mine, will love it. Even those who tell you they don't like salmon will be looking through the lettuce to find more.

Salmon Niçoise

Serve 6

For the Salmon:

6-6 ounce salmon filets (use 3 ounce filets for each serving if making this with a lot of other food for a large party)

Marinate the salmon filets in a mixture of 2/3 cup soy sauce, 2/3 cup good bourbon and 1 cup brown sugar. When ready to cook, preheat oven to 350º and place salmon, skin side down in the pan. Pour a small amount of marinade over the salmon and bake, covered for 30-40 minutes or until salmon is done. Uncover the last 15 minutes of cooking. Remove the skin from the salmon. Refrigerate the salmon being careful not to break the pieces.

3 new potatoes per person—steamed until tender, and chilled
8 green beans per person—steamed until ALMOST DONE and chilled
Green onion stems-steamed-wrap green beans in these in bundles and tie
Grape tomatoes
Cucumbers-sliced and chilled
Black olives-pitted (Kalamata if you can find them)
Boxed organic greens (1 cup greens per person)
Dijon Mustard Vinaigrette

Dijon Mustard Vinaigrette

½ cup white wine vinegar
1 tablespoon whole grain mustard
1 tablespoon lemon juice
2 teaspoons granulated sugar
1 teaspoon Worcestershire sauce
1 teaspoon salt
¼ teaspoon pepper
1 cup olive oil

In a medium bowl, whisk all ingredients except the oil. Add the oil in a slow steady steam, whisking constantly until emulsified with the other ingredients. Taste and add more lemon juice or salt if needed. This dressing will keep refrigerated for up to 4 days. Makes 1-½ cups.

Assembly:

Mound greens on a large platter. Place salmon on the platter with the long end of the salmon filets vertical. Place green bean bundles that have been tied with the green onion stems between the salmon filets. Place the steamed new potatoes around the bottom of the platter. The tomatoes will go above the salmon filets and the cucumbers across the top. Let the olives just fall randomly. Serve the dressing on the side.
Note: Something really good: Mix equal amounts of olive oil, lemon juice and a dash of salt and pepper in a shallow pan. Roll your green beans and potatoes in this mixture before placing on the platter. This gives them an extra depth of flavor.
Note: Olive oil congeals when chilled so remove the vegetables and the salad dressing in plenty of time to "thaw" before serving.

White Bean and Oven-dried Tomato Salad with Mozzarella

This recipe is from Michael Chiarello when we were at The Greenbrier. You can add canned Italian tuna to the salad and make it a meal!

Beans:
1 cup dry cannellini beans or other white beans
½ onion
½ carrot
1 stalk celery
1 quart plus 1 quart cold water
2 cups chicken stock or broth
Salt and pepper to taste
Bay leaf

Place the beans in 1 quart of cold water and bring to a boil. Cover and let cook for 30 minutes. Strain and discard water. Bring the second quart of cold water to a boil with the beans and all of the above ingredients. Simmer slowly until tender. Season the beans with salt and pepper about 15 minutes before done. Remove the bay leaf when beans are done.

Salad:
8 slices mozzarella in water, drained
3 tomatoes that have been oven dried (see recipe below)
¼ cup Italian parsley leaves
1/8 cup olive oil and the juices from the oven-dried tomatoes

Warm the beans with ¼ cup of bean liquid. Add the oven-dried tomatoes until just warm. Take off the heat, toss in oven dried tomato oil and parsley. Arrange on plates, lay slices of fresh mozzarella on top and serve immediately.

Oven-dried tomatoes:

3 fresh tomatoes—cored
8 garlic cloves
4 thyme sprigs
½ cup extra virgin olive oil
2 bay leaves
1-1/2 to 2 tablespoons lemon juice
Salt and pepper to taste

Cut the tomatoes in wedges (sixths). Place the skin side down in a non-reactive baking dish. In a small skillet, heat the olive oil, and garlic cloves until cloves just start to turn light brown. Add the thyme leaves and bay leaves and pour over the tomatoes. Sprinkle with salt and pepper. For best results, bake in a preheated 150º oven for 6 hours or for a quicker preparation, bake in a preheated 250° oven for 3 hours.

Tortellini, Pepperoni Pasta Salad

16 ounces fresh or frozen cheese tortellini
4 ounces chopped salami, or sliced pepperoni
4 ounces provolone or mozzarella cheese, cut into small cubes
1 (11 ounce) can sweet corn, drained
10 ounces fresh spinach washed and chopped or 10 ounces frozen chopped spinach, thawed and squeezed dry
1 cup grape tomatoes
1 (7- ounce) can marinated artichoke hearts, drained and chopped
6 ounces pitted ripe olives cut in half
1-1/2 cups prepared Creamy Italian, or Caesar dressing
1 teaspoon Dijon mustard
½ freshly grated parmesan cheese
1 (2 ounce) jar diced pimiento

Cook tortellini according to package direction. Drain well. Add remaining ingredients and toss to mix. Refrigerate for several hours before serving.
*Make this a real Italian meal and add some imported tuna in oil.

Grilled Chicken Salad with Strawberries & Oranges

The last time I had this salad was on a Summer Sunday when I visited my mother for lunch. This is a salad that she really enjoyed! And, so did I! So much so that I asked for the recipe! She served it with fresh fruit with a sabayon sauce for dessert. Perfect!

Salad:
¾ pound grilled or baked skinless, boneless chicken breast, sliced
2 large oranges, peeled and sections cut away from membrane
2 heads bib lettuce leaves, rinsed and dried
½ cup pecans, toasted or sliced toasted almonds
Fresh strawberries
Dressing

Dressing:
1/3 cup red wine
½ cup sugar
1 cup vegetable oil
1 teaspoon salt
½ onion, finely minced
1 teaspoon ground mustard
¼ teaspoon pepper

Divide the lettuce, chicken, fruit and nuts between 4 salad plates. Mix the dressing ingredients with a wire whisk. Drizzle with dressing. Garnish with fresh strawberries. Makes 4 servings.

Most Favorite Chicken Chutney Salad—The BEST!

From my friend Sue Fonda at Ponte Vedra Beach, FL the best chicken chutney salad you ever put in your mouth!

2 cups diced cooked chicken breast
1 apple peeled, cored, diced
1 small can pineapple chunks, drained
½ cup golden raisins
1 stalk celery, thinly sliced
2 green onions, thinly sliced
½ cups toasted walnuts or sliced almonds
2/3 cup or more of mayonnaise
½ jar Major Grey's mango chutney
½ teaspoon or more curry powder

Mix all ingredients together, blending well. Add more mayonnaise if needed to make the salad very creamy. Serve on a bed of lettuce with a strawberry fan.

Chicken & Wild Rice Salad

4 chicken breast, cooked and cubed
1 small can pineapple tidbits, drained
1 (6-ounce) package long grain and wild rice, cooked according to package directions
1 cup diced celery
¼ cup green pepper
½ cup chopped pecans, toasted
1 tablespoon red wine vinegar
2 tablespoon oil
1 teaspoon salt
¾ teaspoon curry powder
1-1/2 cups mayonnaise or enough to moisten
1 tablespoon dry sherry (optional)

Combine, chicken, pineapple, rice, celery, green pepper, pecans and rice in a large bowl. Whisk together the remaining ingredients and add to chicken. Refrigerate for several hours before serving. Serve in lettuce leaves.

Chilled Shrimp & Red Pepper Pasta

This is a really nice chilled pasta salad. Serve it hot too if you like!

¾ cup bottled ranch salad dressing
1 (3-ounce) package shredded Parmesan cheese (dairy section)
1 box (8-ounces) angel hair pasta
3 tablespoons butter
3 tablespoons olive oil
8 ounces sliced mushrooms
1 pound of peeled, deveined shrimp
1 (12-ounce) jar flame roasted red peppers, drained and cut into strips
½ cup sweet basil leaves cut into thin strips
¼ teaspoon pepper
Salt to taste

Cook pasta according to package directions and drain. Set aside. Melt the butter and sauté the mushrooms until cooked. Add the shrimp and cook for 5 minutes or until done. Drain any liquid from the pan. Combine the hot cooked pasta, olive oil, shrimp and mushrooms. Add the red pepper, basil and black pepper. Toss gently and refrigerate. When ready to serve mix in the salad dressing and parmesan cheese and mix well. Salt to taste.

Shrimp Salad in Tomato Cups

6 tomatoes
1 pound small shrimp, peeled and deveined
1 tablespoon crab boil
2 stalks celery, finely chopped
3 green onions, finely chopped
1/3 cup finely chopped green pepper
¼ cup chopped fresh parsley
2 tablespoons fresh dill, divided (optional)
Mayonnaise

Cover shrimp with water and add 1 tablespoon crab boil. Cook for about 3-4 minutes after water boils, until shrimp are done. Rinse with cold water, drain and chill.
Chop the celery, green onions and green pepper and add to the chilled shrimp. Add 1 tablespoon of the dill and enough mayonnaise to moisten well. Refrigerate until ready to use.
Wash and dry the tomatoes. Cut about 1-inch off the top of the tomato. Reserve the top. Using a spoon, hollow out the inside of the tomato. Salt the inside. Place shrimp salad in the hollowed out tomato and serve on a bed of lettuce. Sprinkle a little dill on top of each salad. Place the slice of tomato that you removed from the top of the tomato back on before serving. Serves 6.

Shrimp & Rice Salad with Curry Dressing

1 cup rice
2 cups chicken broth
3 green onions, thinly sliced
10 large pimiento stuffed olives
1 small bell pepper, chopped
2 ribs celery, thinly sliced
1 (2-ounce) jar pimiento, drained
1 cup petite peas, thawed
1 pound cooked shelled shrimp
1 (7.5 ounce) jar marinated artichokes, chopped

Dressing:
1 cup mayonnaise
1 teaspoon curry
Marinade from artichokes

Cook the rice in the chicken broth. Cool. Mix all ingredients together. Mix dressing ingredients and add to the rice mixture. Refrigerate for several hours before serving.

New Orleans LA Shrimp Remoulade

This is a cooking class favorite. Easy to make and easy to serve.

Dressing:
1/4 cup mayonnaise
¼ cup vegetable oil
3 tablespoons country Dijon mustard
2 tablespoons prepared horseradish
1 tablespoon lemon juice
2 teaspoons chopped fresh parsley
1 teaspoon red wine vinegar
½ teaspoon paprika
2 cloves garlic crushed

Combine the first 9 ingredients in a food processor and process until smooth. Remove to a glass bowl, cover and chill.

Shrimp:
4-1/2 cups water
1 tablespoon salt
1-1/2 tablespoons crab boil—liquid or powder
1 ½ pounds small peeled and deveined shrimp
6 cups shredded lettuce
Red lettuce leaves

Combine water and seasonings in a large pot or Dutch oven; bring to a boil. Add shrimp and cook until shrimp are done, about 5 minutes. Drain well and rinse with cold water. Refrigerate until ready to use.

When ready to serve, combine the Remoulade mixture, shrimp and shredded lettuce. Place on lettuce leaves to serve. Yield: 6-8 appetizer servings.

*Note: If you live in an area where you can get fresh shrimp, please buy 2 pounds small shrimp to peel and cook. If not, then by all means use frozen peeled shrimp with the tails on.

Vegetable Salads

Crunchy Apple Cole Slaw with Creamy Dressing

1 Golden Delicious apple, cored and diced
1 Red Delicious Apple, cored and diced
4 cups finely shredded cabbage
1 (8-ounce) can crushed pineapple, drained
½ cup thinly sliced celery
½ cup chopped pecans, toasted
½ cup raisins

Creamy dressing:
½ cup plain yogurt
½ cup sour cream
½ cup mayonnaise
¾ teaspoon Dijon mustard
½ teaspoon sugar
Pinch of salt and pepper

Combine the apples, cabbage, pineapple, celery, pecans and raisins. Toss lightly with the creamy dressing. Serve on a large platter lined with red lettuce leaves. Serves 8-10.
Creamy dressing:
Combine plain yogurt, sour cream and mayonnaise. Add Dijon mustard, sugar and a pinch of salt and pepper. Thin with milk if too thick.

Asparagus with Balsamic Vinaigrette

This salad is a favorite at Bridal Brunches. It's great served with Putting on the Grits Casserole, a variety of omelets and angel biscuits.

2 pounds asparagus
1/3 cup balsamic vinegar
¼ cup olive oil
Salt and pepper to taste
Herbs of Provence
Orange zest

Wash the asparagus and snap off the woody ends and discard. Even the asparagus spear ends with a knife. Place the asparagus in a shallow skillet. Cover with water. Put on high heat, and cook for 7 minutes from the time you put the skillet on the stove. Asparagus should be crisp tender. Drop the asparagus in ice water to stop the cooking. Dry on a kitchen towel.

Mix balsamic vinegar and olive oil with a whisk. Add salt and pepper to taste.
Place the asparagus on a platter. Pour the vinaigrette over the asparagus. Sprinkle with Herbs of Provence, and orange zest. Sprinkle lightly with salt. Serves 6.

The Best Asian Cole Slaw

Slaw:
1 bag broccoli slaw mix
4 green onions with tender green tops, sliced thin
2 packages (3-ounces each) reserved ramen noodles**
1 cup sliced almonds, toasted

Place broccoli slaw mix, sliced green onions, noodles, and almonds in a large serving bowl. Pour dressing over the slaw mixture and using two forks, toss the mixture until well blended.

Dressing:
1/3 cup white or cider vinegar
4 tablespoons sugar
2 packages (3-ounces each) beef flavored ramen noodle packets*reserve the noodles for the slaw*
1 cup vegetable oil

Mix vinegar, sugar, beef flavoring packets and oil together. Pour over slaw, and mix well when ready to serve.

Best Broccoli Salad

On one of the occasions that I worked on temporary assignment at an Orlando theme park canteen, I was asked to make a salad and this is the recipe that I used. It went out on the salad bar, and was gone in a flash.

2 small broccoli crowns
½ pound bacon, fried or baked until crisp, then crumbled *
3/4 cup red onion chopped
1 cup sliced almonds, toasted or 1 cup sunflower seeds
½ cup raisins
1 cup mayonnaise
¼ cup sugar
2 tablespoons cider vinegar

Cut broccoli flowerets into bite size pieces. Place broccoli, bacon, onion, nuts, and raisins in a large bowl. Mix the remaining ingredients in a small bowl. Pour over the broccoli mixture. Toss. Refrigerate for 3-4 hours until chilled and flavors have mingled. 4-6 servings. *You can buy real bacon pieces in a jar in the grocery store, and use these if you like.

Green pea Salad

1 (16 ounce) Container of frozen baby green peas, thawed
1 (15-ounce) Jar sliced beets, drained (optional)
½ cup finely chopped onion or green onion
1-1/2 teaspoons Dill seasoning (I use a "dilly" seasoning that has lemon in it—by McCormick)
½-1 cup mayonnaise
Salt & pepper to taste

Place frozen peas in a colander and run water over the peas to thaw. Drain well. In a bowl, add peas, drained beets, dilly seasoning, onions, and enough mayonnaise to moisten well. Add salt and pepper to taste. This salad can be made a day ahead, and is even better when refrigerated overnight. Serves 6.

Cornbread Salad

1 cooked skillet (6-8 inches) of cornbread made with Buttermilk Cornbread Mix from recipe on package or your favorite cornbread without sugar
5 green onions including the green tender stems, thinly sliced
¾ cup green pepper
½ cup chopped bread and butter pickles
1 large or 2 small ripe tomatoes, roughly chopped
Mayonnaise to moisten
Salt and pepper to taste

Cook cornbread according to package directions. Put in a large bowl and crumble. Add green onions, bell pepper, pickles, and tomatoes. Add salt and pepper to taste. Add enough mayonnaise to moisten well. Refrigerate until ready to serve. Add crumbled bacon, or anything else you would like to this salad.

Greek Salad

(See Pork tenderloin with Sun-dried Tomatoes, and Greek Potatoes in the index)

2 large tomatoes cut into large cubes or wedges
1 English or hot house cucumber, peeled and sliced
1 red bell pepper, cored, seeded, and sliced into rings
1 large red onion cut into thin wedges
½ pound feta cheese, drained and crumbled
½ cup Kalamata olives, pitted
1 teaspoon chopped fresh parsley
1 tablespoon chopped fresh Greek oregano
½ lemon, juiced
½ cup good olive oil

In a large bowl, combine the tomatoes, cucumbers, bell peppers, onions, and toss well to combine. Crumble the feta cheese over the vegetables and add the olives. Sprinkle with oregano, parsley, and lemon juice and drizzle with the olive oil. Toss again. Serve with bread.

My Grandmother's Potato Salad

Mommy, my grandmother made the best potato salad. This is her recipe or as close to it as I could come since she didn't use a recipe!

4-5 pounds medium red potatoes (or equal pounds baking potatoes)
3/4 cup chopped green onions, or chopped sweet onions
3 hard-boiled eggs, chopped
1 cup celery, finely chopped
½ cup sweet pickle, drained
1 cup mayonnaise or enough to moisten well
1-2 teaspoons yellow mustard or to taste
* I add 1 cup of blanched green beans cut into ¼-inch (tiny) pieces for extra crunch
Salt and pepper to taste

Peel and cube potatoes. Cook until tender and drain. Add the remaining ingredients and refrigerate until ready to serve.
Note: My mother always added celery seed to her potato salad. So if you would like, add 2 teaspoons celery seed to the above recipe.

Mother's Sweet Onion Slaw

Mother loved onions anyway they were prepared. I remember when she used to make onion sandwiches!

3 large sweet onions (about 3-1/2 pounds)
¼ cup white or cider vinegar
¼ cup water
¼ cup sugar
¼ cup mayonnaise
¼ teaspoon celery seeds

Cut onions into very thin slices. Stir together vinegar, water, and sugar until sugar dissolves. Add to onions, tossing gently. Cover and chill 8 hours, stirring occasionally. Drain onion, discarding marinade. Pat the onions dry and return to the bowl. Stir in the mayonnaise and the celery seed. This is great with fish too! Serves 6-8.

Green and Fruit Salads

Baby Lettuce with Caramelized Almonds

Baby greens can be purchased in the grocery store already bagged and triple washed. You will need about 1 cup per person if serving as a salad course. Place greens on a salad plate and top with a couple of tablespoons of the caramelized almonds. Top with Northern Italian Dressing. (I use Ken's Northern Italian Dressing.)
If you are serving a crowd, place the greens on a large platter and sprinkle the nuts over the top, then top with the salad dressing.

Caramelized Almonds

Have a sheet pan ready on the side that has been lined with parchment paper. In a heavy skillet, place 1-1/2 cups of coarsely chopped nuts, I use almonds but you could use pecans or walnuts if you like. Add ½ cup sugar on a medium-low heat and cook the nuts and sugar until the sugar has melted and the nuts have turned light brown in the caramelized sugar. Transfer the nuts to the parchment-lined baking sheet and separate them. Be careful! They will be hot! When the nuts have cooled, place them in an airtight jar or container. Great served on salad, ice cream or as a snack.

Goat Cheese and Pancetta Salad with Winter Greens and Sherry Vinegar

1 tablespoon olive oil
4 ounces pancetta, diced small
2 tablespoons chopped garlic
1 tablespoon chopped thyme
8 ounces goat cheese
4 ounces sherry vinegar
12 ounces mixed winter greens such as spinach, frisee, or arugula
Salt and pepper to taste
1 pear, sliced thin and grilled

Heat the olive oil and pancetta. Add the garlic and brown. Add the thyme and sherry vinegar to deglaze the pan. Cook down slightly. Turn the heat off, and add the crumbled goat cheese, greens, salt and pepper. Toss quickly. Serve warm. Garnish with the grilled pears. Serves 4-6.

Mexican Salad

6 cups shredded or chopped lettuce
1 large ripe tomato, chopped
1 can black beans, drained
1 (11-ounce) can corn, drained
Salsa
2 cups sour cream
½ package taco seasoning mix envelope
¼ cup orange juice

Mix lettuce, tomato, black beans, and corn together in a bowl. Mix sour cream, ½ package taco seasoning mix, and orange juice. Pour over the salad. Top with sliced green onions and tortilla chips.

Citrus Salad with Dijon Mustard Vinaigrette

1 cup assorted greens per person
6-8 Naval Orange sections per person
See index for Dijon Mustard Vinaigrette recipe

Section oranges by slicing off both ends of the orange until you have the meat of the orange. Place the flat side on the cutting board. Take a sharp knife and go down the side of the orange toward the cutting board and cut through the pith of the orange to remove peel. Continue around the orange until it is peeled. Now take your knife and go between the membranes and cut out orange sections. Place the assorted greens on a salad plate or all the greens in a large bowl. Place the oranges on top of the greens. Pour on the vinaigrette.
Note: This salad is also good with thin red onion rings.

Orange & Pear Salad with Grand Marnier & Honey Orange Dressing

This salad is the perfect first course with the Southern White House Chicken.

4 medium size ripe pears, peeled and cored
Lemon juice
1 cup sliced strawberries
3 medium oranges, peeled and sectioned
Mixed baby greens (1 cup per person)
½ cup sliced almonds, toasted or caramelized almonds
Strawberry fans (optional)

Cut each pear into slices, and sprinkle with lemon juice so the pears will not discolor. Mix pears, strawberries, and orange sections. Use about 1 cup of baby greens per person and place the greens on a large platter. Arrange the fruit over the baby greens on the platter. Drizzle salad with Grand Marnier Honey & Orange Dressing. Sprinkle with almonds. If desired, garnish with strawberry fans. Serves 6-8.

Grand Marnier & Honey Orange Dressing

¾ cup honey
½ cup vegetable oil
1/3 cup cider vinegar
2-1/2 tablespoons Grand Marnier
½ teaspoon ground allspice
½ teaspoon orange zest
¼ teaspoon salt
¼ teaspoon dry mustard

Combine all ingredients in a jar; cover tightly, and shake vigorously. Chill thoroughly. Shake well before serving. Serve dressing over salad greens and fruit.

Strawberry, Parmesan Salad with Poppy Seed Dressing

This is another of my favorite salads. I've served it many times in cooking classes and on television shows. I hope you will enjoy this light and delicious salad to keep you cool during the hot days of Southern Summers.

Baby Greens (you can buy them washed and pre-packaged)
You will need 1 cup per person
1/2 cup washed and halved strawberries per person
Freshly grated parmesan cheese
Poppy Seed Dressing (I use Brianna's, available in most grocery stores on the salad dressing aisle)
Place your greens on a platter.
Add the strawberries on top
Sprinkle with the freshly grated parmesan
Pour the desired amount of salad dressing across the top of the parmesan, or place the dressing in a pretty sauce boat or pitcher for pouring separately.
Enjoy!!

Pear & Strawberry Salad

3 cups mixed greens
3 fresh pears sliced and mixed with 1 tablespoon lemon juice
2 cups sliced strawberries
1 bottle Poppy Seed dressing (I use Brianna's)
Fresh Parmesan if you like!

Place greens in a bowl or on a platter. Top with pear and strawberry slices. Toss with Brianna's Poppy Seed dressing. Serves 6.

Southern Pear Salad

This salad was a staple in our house for Sunday dinner. It's still one of my favorites today.

Boston lettuce, washed and dried
1 large can pears or ripe fresh pears (figure 2 halves per person, so buy cans or fresh pears accordingly)
Mayonnaise
Grated Sharp Cheddar

If using fresh pears, make sure you mix them with lemon juice to keep the pears from discoloring. On a platter or pretty plate arrange the lettuce. Place two pear halves per person on each piece of lettuce. Put a teaspoon of mayonnaise in the center of each pear, and sprinkle with cheddar cheese.

Delicious Summer Fruit Salad

1 Red Delicious apple, cored and chopped
1 cup blueberries
1 cup pineapple chunks, drained
1 (11-ounce) can mandarin orange sections, drained
¼ cup raisins
½ cup toasted chopped pecans or sliced almonds
1 tablespoon chopped mint
2 tablespoons sour cream
2 tablespoons light mayonnaise
2 tablespoons Cool Whip or Cool Whip Free

In a medium bowl add the fruit and mint. In a small bowl, blend the mayonnaise, Cool Whip and sour cream. Add to fruit mixture and blend well. Refrigerate until ready to serve. Serves 6.

Chilled Spiced Fruit

Serve in a goblet on a hot summer day. Or use for a brunch buffet.

1 (20-ounce) can pineapple chunks
1 (16-ounce) can sliced peaches
1 (20-ounce) can pear chunks
1 cup sugar
½ cup plus 1 tablespoon vinegar
1 (3-ounce) package cherry gelatin
3 cinnamon sticks
5 whole cloves

Drain pineapple, reserving ¾ cup juice. Drain the peach and pear juices in a bowl and mix gently. Combine the reserved juices, sugar, vinegar, gelatin, cinnamon sticks and cloves in a saucepan. Simmer for 30 minutes, stirring occasionally. Pour over fruit, tossing to mix. Chill covered for 24 hours, stirring occasionally. Discard the cinnamon sticks and cloves. The salad will not congeal. Use fresh fruit, except for pineapple if in season. 10 servings.

Congealed Salads

Orange Congealed Salad

This old Southern salad recipe was given to me by a neighbor in Charleston, many, many years ago. I kept the recipe (handwritten) inside one of my favorite cookbooks so it wouldn't be lost.

1 small can frozen orange juice
2 boxes orange gelatin
2 cans mandarin oranges
1 large can crushed pineapple
2 cups hot water
1 package Dream Whip or equal amount of whipped topping
1 package lemon instant pudding

Mix gelatin and hot water. Add orange juice and chill mixture. Then add fruit. Mix Dream Whip and fold into lemon pudding and spread of top of gelatin fruit mixture. Chill until firmly set.

Spiced Peach Salad

2 (3-ounce) packages lemon gelatin
1 tablespoon plain gelatin
2-1/2 cups boiling water
½ cup lemon juice
1-1/2 cups peach juice
1 (13-ounce) jar spiced peaches, drained
1 cup nuts, chopped and toasted
1 cup celery, chopped

Sour cream dressing:
½ cup sour cream
1 tablespoon chopped parsley
3 tablespoons lemon juice
¼ teaspoon salt
1/8 teaspoon paprika

Add lemon gelatin to boiling water and dissolve. Add lemon and peach juice. Stir well and let set until cool. Add peaches, nuts and celery. Mold until firm. Serve with sour cream dressing.
To make dressing:
Beat sour cream with a fork. Add remaining ingredients. Serve over salad.

Summer Peach Orchard Salad

This is another recipe that Ellen shared with me some years ago.

1 (3-ounce) package lemon gelatin
1 cup boiling water
3 cups diced peaches from 6 fresh peaches
1 cup grape halves
1 cup "free" cool whip

Dissolve gelatin in boiling water. Puree 1 cup peaches. Add to gelatin and cool in the refrigerator for 10-20 minutes. Add cool whip and 2 cups diced peaches and the grapes halves. Put into a mold, or an 8 x 8-inchg dish and chill until set.
Cut squares and serve on a bed of lettuce.

Frozen Apricot Salad

1 (12-ounce) can orange juice
1 juice can water
1 cup sugar
1 (16-ounce) can apricot halves, drained
1 (20-ounce) can crushed pineapple, drained
6 medium bananas, cubed
Lettuce

Line 36 muffin cups with foil liners. Mix frozen orange juice, water and sugar and stir until combined. Chop the apricots into small pieces. Add the apricots, pineapple and banana cubes to the juice mixture. Divide the mixture among the muffin cups, and freeze. When frozen solid, remove the salads to plastic bags to store and put back in the freezer until ready to use. Just prior to serving, remove the foil liner and place on the lettuce lined plates. Work fast, the salads will melt quickly.

Salad Dressings, Cold &
Hot Sauces

French Dressing

½ cup oil
2 tablespoons lemon juice
¾ cup catsup
¼ cup sugar
¼ cup finely chopped or grated onion
2-1/2 tablespoons horseradish
2 tablespoons Worcestershire sauce
¼ cup apple cider vinegar

Mix ingredients together. Refrigerate. Makes 3 cups.

Ginger Dressing for Oriental Salads

1 ounce fresh ginger
1/2 medium onion, chopped
1-1/2 cups vegetable oil
½ cup vinegar
3/4 cup + 2 tablespoons soy sauce
¾ tablespoon tomato paste*
1 teaspoon lemon juice
1 small garlic clove
¾ cup + 2 tablespoons water

Peel ginger with the top of the spoon bowl by scraping the peel off. Divide ingredients in half and process each half in food processor with a steel blade until smooth. Combine both halves. Refrigerate. Makes 4 cups. *You can buy tubes of tomato paste at specialty food stores and store it in the refrigerator.

Steakhouse Honey Mustard Salad Dressing

½ cup mayonnaise
¼ cup honey
2 tablespoons country Dijon mustard

Combine all ingredients in a small bowl. Cover and chill. Serve over your favorite greens.

Park Avenue Mesclun Salad Dressing

¼ cup red wine vinegar
¾ cup balsamic vinegar
2 tablespoons Dijon mustard
4 tablespoons honey
1 teaspoon chopped garlic
1 tablespoon chopped shallots
1 teaspoons fresh cut parsley
1 teaspoons fresh cut basil
1 cup salad oil
1 cup olive oil
½ teaspoon salt
½ teaspoon black pepper

Mix vinegars, mustard, and honey to a smooth paste. Add garlic, shallot and herbs, blend. Slowly whisk in oils. Finish with salt and pepper. Makes 1-1/2 pints. Serve on baby greens.

Red Raspberry Vinaigrette

I have personal chef customers who like this dressing very much!
This dressing is delicious on the Baby Lettuce with Caramelized Almond Salad.

1/3 cup seedless raspberry preserves, or jam
¼ cup vegetable oil
4 teaspoons rice vinegar
4 teaspoons cider vinegar
1 tablespoon dry white wine
1 teaspoon Country Dijon Mustard

In a small bowl, mix the preserves, vinegars, white wine, and mustard. Slowly drizzle the oil into the dressing while whisking. Store in a jar in the refrigerator.

Raspberry Vinaigrette Dressing

¼ cup raspberry vinegar
½ teaspoon Dijon mustard
1 cup olive oil
½ teaspoon salt
¼ teaspoon pepper

Mix the vinegar, mustard, salt and pepper. Drizzle in the olive oil slowly and mix with a wire whisk until the dressing has emulsified.

Lemon Dill Sauce

This sauce is very good with fresh fish.

6 tablespoon butter
6 tablespoons vegetable broth
Juice of 1-1/2 lemons
3 tablespoons freshly chopped dill

In a sauté pan, cook the butter until it begins to froth and brown. Remove from heat. Add the broth and lemon juice and whisk to form a thick sauce. Add the fresh dill. Serve immediately.

Madeira Bleu Cheese Sauce

I have clients who really like this sauce with beef tenderloin. In fact, some of the guest have come into the kitchen and asked how to make it.

3 tablespoons butter, softened
2 ounces blue cheese, crumbled
2 cups beef broth
1 carrot, chopped
1 stalk celery, chopped
3 cloves garlic, minced
3 tablespoons Madeira
½ cup half and half

Combine butter and crumbled bleu cheese; shape into 4 portions, and chill until firm. Combine the beef broth, carrot and celery in a small saucepan. Bring to a boil; reduce heat, and simmer for 5-7 minutes or until broth is reduced to ½ cup. Remove and discard vegetables; set broth aside.
Cook garlic and Madeira in a skillet over medium heat for 2 minutes. Add broth, and cook 3 to 5 minutes or until the mixture is reduced to ½ cup. Gradually stir in half and half, and cook for several minutes or until the sauce is a light brown. Remove sauce from heat. Add blue cheese mixture to the warm sauce a tablespoon at a time, stirring until sauce is smooth. Pour sauce through a wire mesh strainer into a small bowl. Press with the back of a spoon. Makes about 1 cup. Serve over filets or beef tenderloin.

Sweet Jezebel Sauce

This sauce is good cold and served with pork or ham. You can also use the sauce to put over ham during baking.

1 cup apple jelly
1 cup orange marmalade
1 (5-ounce) bottle prepared horseradish from the refrigerated dairy case
1 (6-ounce) jar yellow mustard

Mix all together in an electric mixer and serve in a pretty bowl.

Mustard Barbecue Sauce

Serve this with pulled pork or baked chicken.

½ cup yellow mustard
6 tablespoons sugar
1 cup cider vinegar
2 teaspoons chili powder
2 teaspoons black pepper
½ teaspoon soy sauce
2 tablespoons butter

Combine all ingredients except the soy sauce and butter in a saucepan and simmer for 10 minutes. Remove from the heat. Stir in soy sauce and butter. Place in a jar.

Janice's Delicious Alabama Barbecue Sauce

My dad loves to barbecue pork butts on the grill. When the meat is cooked just right it pulls right off the bone to make a wonderful sandwich. My stepmother, Janice, makes a great barbecue sauce for the pork. The sauce can be served hot or cold. You really won't care how you eat it; you'll just want to eat it!

1 pound brown dark brown sugar
3 garlic cloves, crushed
1 (12-ounce) bottle catsup
1 small jar yellow mustard
1 pint vinegar
1 teaspoon cinnamon
1 teaspoon ground cloves
¼ teaspoon salt
¼ teaspoon pepper

Mix all ingredients together. Simmer for about 20 minutes until all the flavors have had a chance to mix. Store any leftovers in the refrigerator in a jar.

Sauce Au Poivre

This sauce makes the best gravy. If you don't want the peppercorns in, just strain them out.

1 (1-ounce) package (I used Knorr) Peppercorn Sauce Mix
2 tablespoons butter
1-1/4 cup milk (want it really rich—use half heavy cream and half milk)
2 tablespoons brandy

Melt butter and add sauce mix. Whisk in milk. Let sauce come to a boil. Simmer for 1 minute, stirring constantly. Add brandy. Serve over Beef, or pork.

Sauce Au Poivre (2)

1 package (I used Knorr) Peppercorn Sauce Mix
1-1/2 cups water
1 tablespoon chopped shallots
¼ cup dry white wine
3 tablespoons heavy cream
Steak or roast seasoned with salt and coarse black pepper.

In a saucepan, whisk or stir 1-1/2 cups water, and sauce mix until blended. Stirring constantly, bring to a boil over medium-high heat. Reduce heat and simmer, stirring occasionally, 2 minutes. Remove pan from heat, strain, and discard green peppercorns. Keep warm. Season meat of choice, and cook to desired doneness in a sauté pan with least amount of oil. Discard oil but leave drippings of black pepper in pan. Add shallots and dry white wine; reduce volume by half over low heat. Stir in the prepared peppercorn sauce and the heavy cream. Simmer for 5 minutes. Top meat with the sauce. Makes 1-1/2 cups.

Sun-dried Tomato Gravy

2 tablespoon olive or vegetable oil
1 tablespoon all-purpose flour
1 cup half and half
½ ounce sun-dried tomatoes, re-hydrated, drained and finely chopped
1 tablespoon finely chopped green onion
1 tablespoon chopped fresh basil
Salt and pepper to taste

To make the gravy, heat the oil over medium heat. Add the flour and whisk for 1-2 minutes. Add the half and half and stir to thicken. Add the tomatoes, green onion and basil. Season to taste with salt and pepper. Serve gravy over sliced meatloaf.

Brunch, Luncheon, Suppers

Including Soufflés

Sunday Morning Eggs Benedict

Every Sunday morning I used to make Eggs Benedict for my family. I always had to make extra hollandaise sauce because it's sooo good. This is the recipe that I have used for more than 30 years.

You will need English muffins—1 whole muffin per person
Canadian bacon or ham—1 slice for each muffin half
Eggs—1 egg per muffin half
Poached eggs—add a couple of tablespoons of white vinegar to water in a 10- inch skillet. When the water starts to simmer, break the eggs into a small dish and slide the eggs gently into the water from the dish. Cook eggs to desired done-ness. Drain on paper towels before placing the eggs on the English muffins.

My Hollandaise Sauce

¼ cup butter
2 egg yolks, slightly beaten
¼ cup butter, melted
1 tablespoon lemon juice
Pinch salt
Cayenne pepper to taste

Put ¼ cup cold butter and the egg yolks into the top of a double boiler over hot water on medium-low heat. Do not let water boil. Stir until the butter melts. Very slowly, drizzle in the ¼ cup melted butter, whisking while you pour. Stir until the mixture thickens. Add the lemon juice, salt and cayenne pepper. Note: If the mixture breaks or separates, remove from heat, cool down by adding an ice cube, put back on the heat and stir until the mixture comes back together again.

Assembly of Eggs Benedict

Place a toasted English muffin half on the plate. Place a slice of sautéed Canadian bacon or ham on the muffin. Place a poached egg on top of the ham, and spoon hollandaise sauce on top of the egg. Sprinkle with parsley. Serve hot.

Creole Egg Casserole for a Crowd

I've been making this casserole for years. Mother sent me this recipe for a brunch when I lived in Florida. Everyone I've made it for has enjoyed it tremendously.

3 tablespoons butter (Lighten by using olive oil)
1 cup chopped onion
1 cup chopped green bell pepper
2 cloves garlic minced
2 (14.5oz diced tomatoes)
1 teaspoon chili powder
4 tablespoons butter (or olive oil)
4 tablespoons all-purpose flour
2 cups milk (or use 1% milk if you like)
½ teaspoon salt
½ teaspoon pepper
16 hard cooked eggs, sliced (or an equal amount in egg whites)
1 cup shredded cheddar cheese (use a lighter cheese like a 2% for fewer calories)
1 cup soft bread crumbs
2 tablespoons melted butter (use olive oil to lighten)

Melt 3 tablespoons of the butter (or olive oil) in a large skillet over medium high heat. Add onion, bell pepper, and garlic, cook stirring constantly, until tender. Add tomatoes and chili powder, cook on medium-low for 8 minutes and set aside.

Melt 4 tablespoons butter (or olive oil) in a saucepan. Stir in flour and cook two minutes. Gradually stir in milk, salt, and pepper with a wire whisk. Cook mixture 2 minutes or until thick and bubbly. Stir into tomato mixture.

Layer half the egg slices in a lightly greased 13 x 9-inch baking dish or a baking dish large enough to hold the mixture. Top with half the tomato mixture. Repeat layers and sprinkle with cheese.

Combine bread crumbs and 2 tablespoons melted butter (or olive oil). Bake in a preheat 350° oven for about 30 minutes or until bubbly in the center. Let stand 5 minutes before serving.

Serves 12.

Praline Bacon

After mother passed away I was looking through her file of recipes. I found this one and used it for a brunch cooking class. It was a huge hit. I don't know where mother originally got this recipe and I had never eaten it in her home. But, it certainly was worth keeping in her recipe file.

1 pound bacon
4 tablespoons brown sugar
1/3 cup finely chopped pecans

For more spice, sprinkle with chili powder or black pepper.
Arrange bacon on broiler pan. Bake at 400º for 10-15 minutes or until bacon begins to brown. Remove pan from oven and sprinkle bacon with pecans. Continue baking until bacon is crisp.

Bunch of Brunch Eggs

½ pound sliced bacon
2 medium onions, finely chopped
½ stick butter
¼ cup all-purpose flour
1 cup milk
1 cup light coffee cream (half and half)
¼ teaspoon dried thyme
¼ teaspoon dried marjoram
¼ teaspoon dried basil
1 pound grated Swiss, Gruyere or Cheddar cheese
6 hard cooked eggs, sliced
1 pound fresh spinach; chopped, cooked, drained or (10-ounce pkg. frozen chopped spinach)
Buttered fresh bread crumbs

Preheat oven to 350º. Butter an ovenproof baking dish.
Cook bacon until crisp; drain, and crumble. Sauté the onion in bacon drippings. Melt butter in large saucepan over medium heat. Add flour, stirring until mixture is smooth and bubbling. Remove from heat; stir in milk and cream gradually. Return to heat and bring to a boil over medium-high heat, stirring constantly. Boil 1 minute. Reduce heat and add thyme, marjoram, and basil and cheese. Stir until cheese is melted. Layer in prepared baking dish as follows: 1/2 the sauce, 1/2 the eggs, 1/2 the spinach and 1/2 the onion. Reserve a few bacon bits. Sprinkle 1/2 the remaining bacon over onion. Repeat the layers. Sprinkle top with bread crumbs, then sprinkle with reserved bacon and the parsley.

Egg Blossoms with Hollandaise Sauce

6 sheets phyllo pastry, thawed (keep covered with a damp towel to keep from drying out)
6 tablespoons butter, melted
¼ cup grated Parmesan
3 cups chopped baby spinach leaves
12 eggs
Salt and pepper to taste
¼ cup finely chopped green onions
Hollandaise sauce
Cayenne pepper (for garnish)

Lightly brush one sheet of the pastry with the butter. Layer a second sheet on top and brush with the butter. Cut these sheets into 6 equal squares. Repeat the process with the remaining pastry. Stack the 3 squares together, fanning into a spiral. Spray 12 muffin cups with non-stick cooking spray. Press the phyllo spirals into the muffin cups to form a basket. Preheat the oven to 350°. Sprinkle the bottoms of the phyllo cups with spinach and cheese. Break one egg into each cup and season with salt and pepper. Sprinkle the tops with green onion and bake for 20 minutes or until the eggs are set. Remove from oven and place on serving plate. Spoon the hollandaise sauce on each egg cup. Sprinkle lightly with cayenne pepper.

Hollandaise Sauce:

4 egg yolks
3 tablespoons fresh lemon juice
1 stick cold butter

In the top of a small double boiler, whisk together the egg yolks, and lemon juice on low heat. Add 4 tablespoons of the butter and stir constantly until the butter has melted. Add the remaining butter, stirring constantly until the butter has melted and the sauce has thickened. Makes 2 cups.

Spinach & Bacon Frittata

I created this recipe for a Williams Sonoma class.

1 teaspoon olive oil
3 slices bacon, cut into ½ inch pieces
1/3 cup grated Parmigiano-Reggiano cheese
1 small yellow onion, finely diced
½ cup milk
6 whole eggs
Salt and pepper to taste
1 cup shredded Bruder Basil Cheese
2 cups lightly packed spinach leaves, washed of sand, dried

Place olive oil in a large frying pan. Sauté the bacon until crisp. Transfer bacon to a plate and drain. Add onion and sauté until caramelized. Add spinach and sauté until spinach is soft. Add bacon back into the skillet. Break eggs in a bowl, beat the eggs and add milk and Bruder basil cheese. Blend thoroughly. Pour the egg mixture over the spinach, bacon mixture. Move eggs away from the sides of the pan. Add more oil under the egg mixture if needed. At this point you can put the pan into a preheated 350° oven and finish cooking until the eggs are set. When eggs are nearly done, you can add the Parmigiano-Reggiano cheese to the top of the frittata and cook until cheese has melted. Slide the frittata out onto a plate and cut into wedges, or flip over into a plate and serve in wedges. Garnish with fresh herbs and tomatoes.
Note: Bruder basil cheese is a smoky cheese with a smell of basil.

Chevŕe or Stilton Cheese Soufflé

This recipe is from Eric Crane, Executive Pastry Chef at The Greenbrier.

2 cups milk
1 stick butter
1 cup flour
4 ounces Chevŕe or Stilton cheese
5 eggs, separated
¼ teaspoon salt
¼ teaspoon pepper
Thyme

Premix the butter and the flour in a mixing bowl. Heat milk and bring to a boil. Add the butter-flour mixture and beat with a wire whisk to make a roux. Put the mixture into a mixing bowl and start cooling, adding the yolks then. Add small pieces of cheese, salt and pepper. Mix a little more and then remove from the mixer.

In a mixing bowl add the egg whites and beat to make a meringue. Fold into the cheese base. Butter 2 small 1-quart soufflé bowls and place the mixture in the bowls. Sprinkle fresh thyme on top. Bake in a 350º oven until puffed and done, about 30 minutes. Serve immediately.

Grits and Cheese Soufflé

2 cups milk
½ cup quick grits
¼ to ½ teaspoon salt
2 tablespoons butter
½ teaspoon baking powder
3 eggs, separated
½ pound Cheddar cheese, diced into small pieces, or shredded
Salt to taste
Pepper to taste

Heat the milk and salt, and then gradually add the grits. Bring to a boil. Reduce the heat and continue cooking for 2-1/2 minutes or until thickened, stirring constantly. Add butter and baking powder and mix well. Stir small amounts of hot liquid into slightly beaten egg yolks and return to the main mixture.
Add diced or shredded cheese and stir in. Beat the egg whites until stiff peaks form. Fold into the main base.
Pour into a buttered 2 quart casserole or soufflé dish. Bake in a pre-heated 375° oven for about 30 minutes. If there is a sinkhole in the center, it's not done yet.

Beaufort Inn Soufflé

4 slices, buttered bread cut into cubes
3 eggs, lightly beaten
2 cups milk
2 cups finely grated cheese
Salt and pepper to taste
A little chopped basil or thyme would be good too!

Place bread in a baking dish. Mix eggs, milk and cheese, salt and pepper and pour over the buttered bread. Season to taste. Let stand 20 minutes or longer. Bake for 30 minutes in 350° oven, or until set.
4 servings.

Maple Bacon & Swiss Cheese Quiche

½ cup shredded Swiss cheese
1 cup shredded sharp Cheddar cheese, divided
2 tablespoons flour
½ cup cooked maple flavored bacon
2 tablespoons honey mustard *
5 eggs, beaten
1-1/4 cups half and half
¼ cup chopped green onions
¼ teaspoons salt

Line a 9-inch quiche pan or pie pan with pastry. Prick bottom and sides of pastry with a fork. Line pastry shell with parchment paper, fill with beans and bake in a preheated 400º degree oven for 10 minutes. Remove from the oven. Remove the parchment paper and the beans. Set the pastry aside to cool. Combine the Swiss cheese, ½ cup Cheddar cheese and 1 tablespoon flour, and toss gently to coat the cheese with the flour. Place the cooked crumbled bacon on the pastry shell. Place all the Swiss cheese, cheddar mixture on top of the bacon. Combine the eggs, half and half, green onions, 1 tablespoon flour and salt and mix well. Pour the egg mixture over the cheese. Place ½ cup Cheddar over the eggs. Bake at 350º for 40 minutes or until set. Let stand for 10 minutes before serving.
*Note: If you don't have honey mustard, use 1 tablespoon honey and 1 tablespoon mustard.

Herlong Mansion Hash Brown Quiche

I need to thank my cousin Sonny Howard for this wonderful recipe. He used it often at Herlong. He is an excellent cook so I know you will enjoy it!

1 (20-ounce) package refrigerated or frozen shredded hash browns
1/3 cup melted butter
4 cups shredded mild Cheddar cheese
6 cups milk
12 eggs
Cayenne pepper and garlic salt

Preheat the oven to 425º Use 6 per "Texas size" muffin pan. (This would mean jumbo muffin pan). Press hash browns into the muffin cups to form a crust. Brush or drizzle with the melted butter. Bake for 25-30 minutes. Reduce the oven temperature to 350°. Fill crust with cheese.
Whisk together the milk, eggs, pepper and salt. Pour into muffin cups and bake 30-40 minutes or until toothpick inserted in center comes out clean. Makes 12 servings. Allow to cool before removing from the pan.

Savory Summer Pie

Ellen called to say that she had this wonderful quiche and I needed to try it. She was right as usual; it is delicious and good for brunch, lunch or supper.

1 refrigerated pie crust
¾ cup chopped bell pepper
½ cup chopped purple onion
2 garlic cloves, minced
2 tablespoons olive oil
2 tablespoons chopped fresh basil or 1 tablespoon dried
4 large eggs
1 cup half and half
1 teaspoon salt
½ teaspoon pepper
2 cups shredded Monterey Jack cheese
½ cup shredded Parmesan
3 plum tomatoes cut into ¼ inch- slices

Place the pie crust into a 9-inch deep dish tart pan; prick the bottom and sides of the crust with a fork. Place a piece of parchment paper inside the pie crust. Fill with beans.
Bake at 425º for 10 minutes. Remove the paper and beans. Set aside. Reduce heat to 375°.
In a large skillet, sauté the bell pepper, onion and garlic in the olive oil for about 5 minutes. Stir in the basil. Whisk the eggs in a large bowl. Add the half and half, salt and pepper. Add the onion mixture and the cheese. Pour into the pie crust and place the sliced tomatoes on top. Bake at 375° for 45 minutes or until set. Let stand for several minutes before serving so it will be easier to slice. 8 servings.

Shrimp & Grits Casserole

1 cup quick cooking grits (not instant)
4 cups milk
½ to 1 teaspoon salt
1 pound medium peeled, deveined shrimp
¼ cup chopped onion
¼ cup chopped green pepper
3 tablespoons olive oil
2 teaspoons roasted garlic (available in a jar at your grocery store) or 2 teaspoons chopped garlic
½ teaspoon red pepper flakes
2 tablespoons fresh lemon juice
2 cups sharp cheddar (2% cheese if fine)
Salt and pepper to taste

Bring 4 cups of milk, and salt to a boil. Whisk in grits, and cook on medium—low for about 5 minutes or until grits are done, and most of the liquid is absorbed. Salt to taste. (Add more milk if the grits get to dry). Heat the oil in a skillet over medium heat; add the onion, pepper, shrimp, roasted garlic, red pepper flakes, and lemon juice. Cook for about 5 minutes or until shrimp are cooked through. Add the shrimp mixture, and 1-1/2 cups of the cheese to the grits mixture. Salt and pepper to taste. Pour into a greased casserole. Spread the remaining ½ cup cheese on top. Bake in a preheated 350º oven until hot and bubbly (25-30 minutes). Yield: Six (1-cup servings.) *Add 2 tablespoons butter for a richer casserole.

Garlic Cheese Grits

4 cups water
1 cup quick cooking grits (not instant-I use the grits with the Quaker on the front)
½ teaspoon salt
1 (6 ounce) roll process cheese food with garlic
Dash of cayenne pepper

Bring water to a boil and whisk in grits and salt. Return to a boil, cover and reduce the heat to low. When cooked, add the cheese and pepper stirring until the cheese melts. Serves 6. (Maybe.)

Putting on the Grits & Sausage Casserole!

1 pound mild pork sausage
1 pound hot pork sausage * use two packages mild if you don't like hot
4 cups water
1-1/4 cups quick grits, uncooked (not instant grits!)
4 cups shredded Cheddar cheese
1 cup milk
½ teaspoon dried thyme
1/8 teaspoon garlic powder
4 large eggs

Brown sausage in a large skillet, stirring until it crumbles. (A good way to crumble the sausage is to use a potato masher while it's cooking.) Drain well and set aside. Bring water to a boil in a large saucepan. Whisk in grits. Return to a boil, cover and reduce heat. Simmer for 5 minutes, stirring often. Remove from heat. Add the cheese, sausage and remaining ingredients, stirring until the cheese melts. Bake in a 13 x 9 inch oven proof baking dish for 35-45 minutes at 350º, or until hot and bubbly all the way through.

Note: This casserole can be prepared ahead and kept refrigerated overnight. Remove from the refrigerator and let stand at room temperature for 30 minutes before baking.

Sherried Fruit Casserole

1 (20-ounce) can sliced pineapple
1 (17-ounce) can apricot halves
1 (16-ounce) can peach halves
1 (16-ounce) jar pear halves
1 (14.5-ounce) jar spiced apple rings (or 1 large can Royal Anne Cherries, drained)
1 can maraschino cherries, drained
1 stick butter
½ cup brown sugar
1 tablespoon cornstarch
1 cup dry sherry

Drain the first 5 ingredients. Combine fruit in a 2-quart casserole dish; set aside. Melt the butter in a small saucepan over medium heat. Combine the sugar and cornstarch. Add this to the melted butter stirring constantly. Add the sherry and cook, stirring constantly until the mixture thickens. Pour the sherry mixture over the fruit, decorate the top with maraschino cherries and bake in a 350° pre-heated oven for 35 minutes or until bubbly. Serves 8.

Long Island Blintz Casserole

Serve this dish with assorted jams, or fresh fruit.

Casserole:
1-1/2 cups low fat sour cream
½ cup orange juice
1 tablespoon orange zest
1 stick butter, softened
1 cup flour
1/3 cup sugar
6 eggs
2 teaspoons baking powder

Cream Cheese Filling:
1 (8-ounce) cream cheese softened
2 cups small-curd cottage cheese
1 egg
2 tablespoons sugar
1 teaspoon vanilla

Filling: Combine the cream cheese, cottage cheese, egg, sugar, and vanilla in a food processor container fitted with a steel blade. Process until blended. Set aside.
Casserole: Combine the sour cream, orange juice, zest, butter, flour, sugar, eggs and baking powder in blender or food processor fitted with a steel blade. Process until blended. Spread ½ the batter in a buttered 13 X 9-inch baking dish. Drop the cream cheese filling by heaping tablespoons over the prepared layer. Spread evenly with a knife; it will mix slightly with the batter. Top with the remaining batter. Bake at 350º for 50 to 60 minutes or until puffed and golden. Serve immediately with additional sour cream and your favorite fruit syrup or assorted jams. You may prepare several hours or one day in advance and store covered in the refrigerator. Bring to room temperature before baking. Serves 8.

Decadent French Toast Casserole with Praline Syrup

This recipe was e-mailed to me by a friend of my son Ed. Her name is Lynn Young and she lives in Charleston. Thanks, Lynn for a really great recipe.

1 loaf French bread (baguette)
8 large eggs
2 cups half and half
1 cup milk
2 tablespoons sugar
1 teaspoon vanilla extract
¼ teaspoon ground cinnamon
¼ teaspoon ground nutmeg
Dash of salt
Praline Topping
Maple syrup

Slice the French bread into 20 slices, 1-inch thick. Generously butter a 13 x 9-inch oven proof baking dish. Arrange slices in two rows, overlapping the slices. In a large bowl, combine the eggs, half and half, milk, sugar, vanilla, cinnamon, nutmeg and salt and beat with a wire whisk until blended but not bubbly. Pour mixture over the French bread slices, making sure that all slices are covered evenly with the mixture. Cover and refrigerate.
The next day, preheat the oven to 350° Spread praline topping evenly over the bread and bake for 40 minutes. Serve with maple syrup.

Praline Topping:
2 sticks butter
1 cup packed light brown sugar
1 cup chopped pecans
2 tablespoons light corn syrup
½ teaspoon cinnamon
Light sprinkling of nutmeg
Combine all ingredients in a medium bowl and blend well.

Herlong Mansion Decadent Bread

1 loaf French bread
2 eggs
¾ cup granulated sugar
3 cups (2 %) milk
1 cup half and half
1 stick melted butter
1 tablespoon vanilla extract
Nutmeg and Cinnamon

Preheat oven to 350°. Slice French bread 1-1/2 inches thick and place in a large baking dish or ramekin. Pour mixture of eggs, sugar, milk, half and half, butter, vanilla, nutmeg and cinnamon over the bread. Allow 5 minutes to soak. Then turn the bread over and refill to ¾ level. Garnish with fresh fruit and bake for 45 minutes. Serve with walnuts, syrup and sausage on the side. 6 servings.

Herlong Mansion Refrigerated Pineapple Bran Muffins

I usually make half of this recipe at a time, and freeze the muffins until I am ready to use them. The full recipe is below.

1 (20-ounce) box raisin bran cereal
3 cups sugar
5 cups flour
5 teaspoons soda
2 teaspoons salt
1 cup walnut pieces
1 quart buttermilk
1 (20-ounce) can crushed pineapple, undrained
4 eggs
1 cup vegetable oil

Pour the box of raisin bran into a large bowl. Add the sugar and stir. Sift flour, soda, and salt into the cereal. Add walnuts and stir.

In a separate large mixing bowl, mix buttermilk, pineapple, eggs and vegetable oil. Stir until completely mixed. Then pour contents into dry mixture and completely stir. The final mixture should be in a container with a top. The mixture can be refrigerated for up to 6 weeks. Bake in mini-muffin tins which have been greased and cook muffins at 350° for 17 minutes.

Coffee Cake

My neighbor in Charleston gave me this recipe about 35 years ago. I still make it after all these years. The smell of this cake cooking makes me want to eat the whole thing by the time it comes out of the oven.

Cake:
2 cups flour
½ cup butter
2 eggs
1 cup sugar
1 teaspoon baking powder
1 teaspoon baking soda
½ teaspoon salt
1 cup sour cream
1 teaspoon vanilla

Nut Topping:
½ cup light brown sugar
¼ cup white sugar
1 teaspoon cinnamon
¼ cup chopped pecans, toasted

Cream butter and sugar until light and fluffy. Add eggs one at a time. Add the dry ingredients and the sour cream, beginning and ending with the flour mixture. Pour ½ the batter into a 10" tube pan. And cover with ½ of the cinnamon, sugar, nut filling. Add the remaining batter and cover with the remaining nut mixture. Bake in a 325º preheated oven for 40 minutes. Dot the top of the cake with butter after you take it out of the oven.

Sandwiches and Pizza

Ham Stuffed Sandwich

1 large round loaf of rosemary, or herb sourdough bread
1 (6-ounce) jar pitted black or pitted Kalamata olives, drained
1 large garlic clove, minced
2 tablespoons olive oil
½ pound black forest ham, thinly sliced
1 large jar flame roasted pimiento peppers, drained
1 cup fresh basil leaves
Sliced tomatoes

Using the tip of a knife, cut into the top of the bread round in a large circle. Cut almost to the bottom of the bread round. Hollow out the inside of the bread. Remove the top, cut the inside of the top off flat to about one inch of the underside of the top, so that it will fit flat back on the sandwich and set aside.
Place the garlic clove and olives into a food processor with the olive oil. Blend to finely chop.
Spread this mixture inside the bread round, and under the top of the bread. Spread the remainder of the mixture on the underside of the top of the bread. Place one layer of red pimiento peppers in the bottom of the round. Place half the ham over the pepper, then top with half the tomato slices, and half the basil leaves. Repeat layers. Replace the lid. Cover tightly and refrigerate so that flavors can come together. Refrigerate for about an hour before serving. Serves 6.

Pork Tenderloin Sandwich with Caramelized Onions and Apple Butter

3 tablespoons butter
4 cups thinly sliced onions
1/4 teaspoon dried thyme
2 tablespoons balsamic vinegar
¼ cup apple butter
¼ cup country Dijon mustard
Thick sliced pork tenderloin to cover length of sandwich
8 slices Muenster cheese or horseradish Cheddar cheese
1- (16-ounce) French bread or long baguette

Heat butter in a large skillet to a sizzle. Add onions and thyme and cook, stirring frequently until onions are golden brown or caramelized, and cooked through. Add balsamic vinegar. Let simmer until vinegar is slightly reduced. Set aside to cool.
Mix the apple butter and the mustard.
Halve the bread lengthwise and spread each side with the apple butter mixture. Arrange pork tenderloin along the bread slice. Top with caramelized onions and then cheese. Place halves back together. Cut on the diagonal. Or place whole sandwich in the refrigerator tightly wrapped in foil until ready to serve. You can warm in the oven if too cold. Serves 6-8.

Becca's Hawaiian Pizza

Rebecca, my granddaughter, came to visit during Christmas vacation.
She made pizza for dinner one night. It was delicious. She is only 8, but loves to cook.

1 pre-prepared pizza dough
1 can prepared pizza sauce
2 cups slivered ham
1 cup pineapple tidbits, drained
Mozzarella cheese
4 tablespoons sliced basil
Parmesan cheese
Olive oil

Preheat oven to 425º, or whatever temperature the pre-pared dough package gives instructions for. Spread pizza dough to desired thickness on pizza pan or baking sheet. Rub the dough with olive oil. (This keeps the sauce from seeping through the dough and making it soggy). Spread the desired amount of pizza sauce on the dough. (Rebecca used ½ can of the sauce). Sprinkle with mozzarella cheese. Sprinkle with ham and pineapple. Bake for 30 minutes or until dough is done and cheese is bubbly. Sprinkle with parmesan cheese.

Becca's Goat Cheese Pizza

This is Rebecca's favorite pizza. She made the goat cheese pizza for the first time on her holiday visit and discovered that she "loves" goat cheese!

1 pre-prepared pizza dough
Olive oil
1 can prepared pizza sauce
1 small roll of goat cheese
4 tablespoons sliced basil

Preheat oven to 425°. Roll out dough to desired thickness onto a pizza pan or baking dish. Rub the dough with olive oil. Spread with half the can of pizza sauce. Break up the goat cheese and place on the sauce, and sprinkle with the sliced basil. Bake pizza until goat cheese is bubbly and dough has cooked through.

Tomato, Pepperoni, Cheese Galette

¾ pound purchased puff-pastry
1 tablespoon olive oil
1 small onion, finely chopped
2 garlic cloves, finely chopped
1 (14.5) ounce can diced Italian tomatoes
1 tablespoon tomato paste
2 teaspoons Greek oregano, finely chopped plus fresh leaves for garnishing
½ cup sliced pitted Kalamata olives
4 ounces thinly sliced mozzarella
¼ cup freshly grated Parmesan cheese

On a lightly floured surface, roll out the puff pastry to make a 10 or 11-inch circle. Slide the circle onto a lightly floured baking sheet. Prick the bottom all over. Refrigerate for 30 minutes.

In a medium skillet over medium-high heat, heat the oil. Add the onion and cook stirring occasionally, until the onion gets soft and golden. Add the garlic and cook for 1 minute more. Stir in the tomatoes, tomato paste, and oregano. Cook until the sauce is thickened and reduced, about 10-15 minutes. Season with salt and pepper. Remove from the heat to cool.

Preheat the oven to 400º. Wrap a 10-inch diameter plate with foil and center it over the pastry. Weigh it with baking beans and blind bake the pastry for 10 minutes. Remove the plate and bake for 2 minutes more.

Spread the cooled tomato sauce evenly over the pastry circle to within ½-inch of the edge of the pastry. Arrange the pepperoni slices evenly over the top. Sprinkle with the fresh oregano leaves, and olives. Spread the mozzarella cheese on top. Sprinkle with Parmesan cheese. Bake until the pastry is crisp and the cheese is bubbling, about 10 minutes. Cover with foil if the top starts to brown before the pizza has cooked.

Note: You can also make this galette a tart by placing the round of dough to fit a tart pan. Blind bake the dough in the tart pan, and then follow the same directions above.

Soups & Stews

Winter Memories & Sarah's Soup

When the cold of a South Carolina winter finally starts to creep under the door, it's time to warm up with a bowl of hot soup and good corn bread. And, I don't know about you, but I feed my southern soul with the soup that was my favorite as a child back in my native Alabama.

Our family had a cook when I was growing up in the 1950's and 60's. We were lucky. Her name was Sarah. She was not only our cook, but also our caretaker and our friend. Sarah died in the early 1970's. I missed her terribly, and I longed for the taste of her food, and her loving care. On cold winter days, Sarah made the most wonderful vegetable beef soup. I tried for years to make Sarah's soup with no luck. She would add a little corn and some okra, and tomatoes along with a few soup bones and then magic would happen right there in the kitchen of our old house!

Back in those days my mother didn't cook very much unless it was around the holidays. Sarah was responsible for our every day meals. Even though my mother was an excellent cook, she didn't cook with recipes either. So, I was on my own to discover the long lost soup recipe.

A few years ago, while I was researching recipes on soups for a cooking class, I came across one that I wanted to try for vegetable beef soup. It looked good, but it had too many ingredients. So, I modified it to fit today's lifestyle. It seems that today's cooks want the same taste of the old days, but with the convenience of today. Lo and behold! In modifying that recipe I had found Sarah's soup! The exact taste that I was longing for.

It was like going home. Along with the soup, I made some cornbread with white cornmeal, not yellow, and had a feast by the fire. I was warm inside and out. I guess what I had really found was a homecoming in that wonderful bowl of soup. Thank goodness!

My grandfather used to sing this song, "How you gonna keep 'em down on the farm, after they've seen Paree." Well, I went to French cooking school, but I still love my south, and I still love my southern cooking! And, I'm still gonna have okra in my soup!

I'd like to share Sarah's vegetable beef soup recipe with you. Don't forget to make some good cornbread to go along with it. Light the fire, and curl up on the sofa with your bowl of hot soup.

Sarah's Vegetable Beef Soup

2 pounds ground sirloin
¼ cup butter
¼ cup flour
6 cups water
1 (16-ounce) package soup vegetables with okra
1 (16-ounce) package vegetable gumbo mix
1 (28-ounce) can diced tomatoes
1 (15-ounce) can tomato sauce
3 tablespoons beef granules or beef flavoring base
1-1/2 teaspoons salt or to taste
Pepper to taste

Brown the beef in a large stockpot or soup pot. Add the butter and let it melt, and then add the flour. Cook for several minutes to cook the flour. Add the water and the beef granules. Add the remaining ingredients. Simmer uncovered for 1 to 1-1/2 hours. Makes about 13 cups. The soup freezes well.

Cream of Asparagus Soup

1 pound asparagus spears
1 (14-ounce) can chicken broth
2 tablespoons butter
2 tablespoons flour
½ cup sour cream
1 cup milk
1 teaspoon lemon juice
1 teaspoon salt
Pinch of freshly ground black pepper

Wash asparagus to remove any sand. Snap asparagus at the tender end. Discard the tough end. Cut the asparagus into 1-inch pieces. In a medium saucepan, cook the asparagus in ½ cup chicken broth until the asparagus is tender, about 10-12 minutes. When the asparagus is done, remove the broth and asparagus to a food processor and puree (or use a hand held emulsifier).
In a saucepan, melt the butter over medium heat. Add the flour and cook, whisking for 2 minutes. Do not brown. Gradually add the remaining chicken broth, stirring constantly. Bring the heat up to boiling until mixture starts to thicken. Stir in the asparagus puree and the milk. Put the sour cream in a bowl, and gradually add some of the soup mixture to warm it. Then add the sour cream mixture and the lemon juice into the soup. Reduce heat and continue to cook until the soup reaches serving temperature. Do not allow the soup to boil the second time. Add salt and pepper. Serves 4-6.
Note: Milk and sour cream will separate when cooked too fast. So go slow with this one.

Cream of Broccoli Soup

Follow the directions for Cream of Asparagus but use 2 cups of Broccoli with Cheese Sauce from the large bag of Green Giant Broccoli in Cheese Sauce. (This is the Green Giant product that has the pieces of broccoli and the chunks of cheese sauce frozen in the bag). Cook the broccoli and cheese in the chicken broth until tender. Follow the same directions as the Cream of Asparagus soup. You may not want to add the lemon juice.

The Best Black Bean Soup

3 tablespoons olive or vegetable oil
2 cups chopped red onion
2 garlic cloves, finely chopped
1 (4-ounce) can chopped green chilies
1 tablespoon chopped fresh jalapeno
1 tablespoon ground cumin
2 (15-ounce) cans seasoned black beans, undrained (it will say seasoned on the can)
2 cups chicken broth
8 tablespoons chopped fresh cilantro
Sour cream

Heat the oil in a Dutch oven over medium high heat. Add onions, garlic, green chilies, jalapeno and cumin. Cook until onions are tender. Add the beans and chicken broth and bring soup to a boil. Cover and reduce heat to simmer until flavors are blended about 20 minutes. Puree 3 cups of the soup in a food processor or blender. Return to the pot. Add cilantro. Serve with sour cream and tortilla chips if desired.

Emily's Favorite Cream of Chicken Soup

My granddaughter Emily was not feeling well. I called to cheer her up. She asked me for a chicken soup recipe and this is the one I gave her!

1-1/2 sticks unsalted butter
¾ cup flour
1 cup warm milk
6 cups hot chicken broth, divided
1 cup warm half and half
1-1/2 cups chopped cooked chicken
¾ teaspoons salt
Pepper to taste

Melt the butter in a Dutch oven over low heat. Stir in the flour and cook until smooth and bubbly. Combine the milk, 2 cups chicken broth and half and half. Gradually add to the flour mixture. Cook and stir until well blended. Add the remaining 4 cups broth, chicken and salt and pepper. Heat thoroughly.

Sopa Santa Fe

2 pounds ground sirloin
1 large onion, chopped
2 (1-ounce) packages ranch style dressing mix
2 (1.25-ounce) envelopes taco-seasoning mix
1 (16-ounce) can black beans, undrained
1 (16-ounce) can kidney beans, undrained
1 (16-ounce) can pinto beans, undrained
1 (16-ounce) can diced tomatoes with chilies, undrained
1 (14.5-ounce) can diced tomatoes
1 (16-ounce) cans white corn, undrained
2 cup water
Sour cream, shredded cheese, green onions, tortilla chips

Cook the ground sirloin and onion together until the meat is browned. Stir in the ranch dressing mix and the taco seasoning mix. Add the bean, tomatoes and corn with their juices. Add the water and simmer for 2 hours. If the mixture becomes too thick, add water. Serve with the sour cream, cheese and green onions. Top with tortilla chips.

Sweet Cream of Corn Soup

3 tablespoon unsalted butter
1 cup chopped onion
1/2 cup shredded carrot
1 (16-ounce) pkg. Birdseye Sweet Kernel Corn
3 cups chicken broth
4 tablespoons butter
4 tablespoons flour
2/3 cup fat free or regular half and half
Salt to taste
Pepper to taste
Cayenne pepper to taste (I use just a dash)

In a Dutch oven, melt 3 tablespoon butter. Sauté the onion and carrot in the butter until onions have started to become translucent. Add the corn and chicken broth and bring to a boil. Reduce to a simmer and cook for 8-10 minutes or until corn is very tender. In the meantime, melt the 4 tablespoons butter in a small saucepan and stir in flour, whisking constantly. When the flour mixture has cooked for 2-3 minutes, add it to the simmering corn mixture. Use an emulsifier to puree the corn mixture, or place it a few cups at a time in the food processor and process until smooth. Add it back to the Dutch oven. It will not be totally smooth. Add the half and half into the soup mixture and cook gently for 3-4 minutes more, or until soup has thickened. Serves 6.

Chicken & Ham Chili with Black-Eyed Peas & Rice

Serve for a New Year's Day luncheon, or supper.

2 tablespoon olive oil
1 large onion, chopped
1 garlic clove, minced
1 cup cubed ham
1 pound boneless, skinless chicken breast, cut into ½-inch cubes
2 cups cooked long grain and wild rice or cooked white rice
1 (15.8 ounce) can black eyed peas, drained
1 (11-ounce) can shoepeg corn, drained
2 (4-ounce) cans chopped green chilies
1 (14.5 ounce) can chicken broth
1 teaspoon ground cumin
2 teaspoon chili powder
1 teaspoon salt
Chopped green onions, jack cheese for garnish

In a Dutch oven, heat the olive oil. Add the onion, garlic, ham and chicken. Cook, stirring often until the chicken has lost its pink color.
Add the remaining ingredients except the onions and cheese. Simmer for 30 minutes until all flavors have had a chance to blend.
Add green onions and cheese as a garnish.

White Bean Chicken Chili

Chili is chili you say! This is a good little chili and easy to make.

1 medium onion, finely chopped
3 tablespoons olive oil
1 (4-ounce) can chopped green chilies
3 tablespoons all purpose flour
2 teaspoons ground cumin
2 (15.8 ounce) cans Great Northern Beans
1 (14.5 ounce) can chicken broth
1- 1/2 cups chopped cooked chicken breast
Shredded Monterey Jack cheese
Sour cream
Salsa

In large skillet, cook onion in oil for 4 minutes or until transparent. Add chilies, flour and cumin. Cook and stir for 2 minutes. Add beans and chicken broth; bring to a boil. Reduce heat; simmer for 10 minutes or until thickened. Add chicken, cook until hot. Garnish with cheese, sour cream and salsa.

My favorite Turkey Chili

I love this chili! And, so does everyone that I make it for.

2 tablespoon vegetable or mild olive oil
1/3 cup chopped onion
1/3 cup chopped celery
1/3 cup chopped bell pepper
1 tablespoon roasted garlic (found in the produce section)
OR use 2 teaspoons fresh garlic
1 (20-ounce) package ground turkey
1 (1.25-ounce) packet chili seasoning mix
1 (10-ounce) can milder diced tomatoes and green chilies
1 (16-ounce) can chili beans (undrained)
1 (8-ounce) can tomato sauce
Shredded cheddar or Monterey Jack (optional for topping)
Sour cream (optional for topping)

In a large saucepan, heat the olive or vegetable oil on medium-high heat. Add onion, celery, pepper and garlic. Cook 6-8 minutes, stirring often. Reduce heat to medium; brown ground turkey 5-7 minutes stirring until it crumbles and is well browned. Stir in remaining ingredients. Bring to a boil; reduce heat to low and simmer 10-12 minutes, stirring occasionally, until thoroughly heated and flavors are well blended.

Turkey or Chicken and Wild Rice Chili

1 tablespoon olive oil
1 onion, chopped
1 garlic clove, minced
1-1/4 pounds boneless, skinless chicken or turkey, cut into ½-inch pieces
2 cups cooked wild rice
1 (15-ounce) can Great Northern Beans, drained
1 (11-ounce) can white corn, drained
2 (4-ounce) cans diced green chilies
1 (14.5-ounce) can chicken broth
1 teaspoon ground cumin
2 teaspoons chili powder
1 teaspoon salt
Monterey Jack or Sharp Cheddar cheese
Sour cream
Chopped cilantro (optional)

Heat the oil in a large skillet or Dutch oven over medium heat. Add the onion and garlic and sauté until tender. Add the turkey, (or chicken), wild rice, corn, beans, chilies, chicken broth, cumin, chili powder and salt. Cover and simmer over medium-low heat for 30 minutes or until turkey (chicken) is tender and thoroughly cooked. Serve with cheese and sour cream. Garnish with cilantro.

Cream of Portabella Mushroom Soup

1 cup chopped green onions
1 (8-ounce) package chopped baby portabella mushrooms
3 tablespoons butter
3 tablespoons flour
2 cups milk or 2 cups fat free half and half
1 cup chicken broth

In a large saucepan, sauté green onions and mushrooms in the butter until the mushrooms are cooked. Stir in flour and cook for about 2 minutes more. Gradually add the milk and broth to the mixture, stirring well. Cook over low heat for 10 minutes or until thoroughly heated and thickened, stirring constantly.
Puree in a blender, food processor or a hand-held emulsifier. 4 servings.

Winter Tomato Soup

3 tablespoons olive oil
1 cup chopped sweet onion, such as Vidalia
9 large Roma tomatoes
4 stems fresh thyme or ½ cup basil leaves
1 cup tomato juice (I used organic)
Kosher salt to taste
Black pepper

In a large Dutch oven, sauté the onion in the oil until tender. Chop the tomatoes and add to the onion. Add the tomato juice. Add the thyme or basil, salt and pepper, and cook, covered on low heat until tomatoes are cooked. Using a hand held blender, puree the soup, or if you don't have a hand held blender, process the soup in a food processor with a steel blade or use a food mill. Strain. Add salt and pepper to taste. Place back into a heavy pan and reheat. Serve with garlic croutons. Serves 4.

Mother's Winter Tomato Basil Soup

I believe that mother found this recipe when she went out to California.

2 ½ pounds of peeled, seeded and cut up tomatoes (6 cups) or in winter use 2 (1 pound) can tomatoes, undrained
1/3 cup lightly packed fresh basil leaves or 1-1/2 tablespoons dried basil
1 cup chicken broth
1 tablespoon sugar
¼ teaspoon salt
¼ teaspoon pepper
¼ teaspoon red pepper

In a food processor, place half of the undrained canned tomatoes (or the cut-up tomatoes) and all of the basil. Process until smooth. Repeat the process of pureeing the remaining tomatoes. Add the pureed tomatoes to a large saucepan. Stir in chicken broth, sugar, salt and peppers. Bring to boiling and then reduce heat. Cover and simmer for 30 minutes. Serve immediately or transfer to a covered container and refrigerate. Makes 6 (3/4 cup) servings.

Vegetables & Side Dishes

Growing up in the Country

We lived in a little town in the country when I was growing up. We were 15 miles from the nearest town of any size, and 21 miles from the county seat. Back then, snacks would be something like a jar of homemade fig preserves on crackers under a honeysuckle vine or tea cakes and lemonade.

There was not a thought of potato chips or any other snack from the store unless it was ice cream. And, for dinner and supper we had meat, fish or chicken and lots of vegetables.

There was a vegetable truck that came around from Mobile. It had a canopy to cover the vegetables and keep them cool, and scales for weighting on the back of the truck. The truck driver went to each house and knocked at the door to see if the cooks or housewives would like to buy what was not available in local gardens. There was not a shortage of good food available. I remember the old truck vividly as it parked under the two giant oaks in front of our house.

The days of vegetable trucks are long gone. But fortunately you can visit your local market for some fresh farm produce. Or even produce from different parts of the world.

It's not only enjoyable to visit local markets and purchase fresh butter beans or corn, but it's good for the soul. It's a reminder of days past and things good. These days I'll drive up on Highway 25 on Saturday morning and visit some of the markets that carry local produce, especially, tomatoes and corn.

Often I will get there about the same time as the truck loaded with the corn and the corn is so fresh you could eat it on the cob right there at the market.

I'll buy butter beans, okra, tomatoes and corn, my favorite foods for a good old country dinner. Since my husband is from New York, and did not grow up in the country or eat the same kind of food, then I am left alone to eat my bounty. And, relish it I do! Sometimes I don't have a meat entrée, just the vegetables and some corn bread salad.

Corn bread salad is good! (See index). It has all of the ingredients in it that go well with the vegetables if you were eating them alone. Every time I make this recipe or include it in one of my cooking classes, it's a big hit. I'm sure some of you have made this dish during the summer, and may already have your favorite recipe for cornbread salad. But, like me you may forget occasionally how good it really is. And, others of you who want a taste of the Southland will want to try it. Enjoy the salad, enjoy the summer! I'll see you while I'm out looking for just plain good food!

Apricot Casserole

I made this recipe for my Anderson cooking class and it was at the top of their list for favorites.

4 (15.25-ounce) cans unpeeled apricot halves in syrup, well drained
30 Ritz crackers, crushed
1-1/2 cups brown sugar, firmly packed
1 teaspoon cinnamon
1 stick of butter, melted

Preheat the oven to 350º. Layer half the apricots in a greased 2 quart oven-proof casserole dish. Combine the crackers, sugar and cinnamon. Put half of the cracker mixture over the apricots. Repeat the layer. Pour melted butter over the top and bake for 30 minutes.

Asparagus & Deviled Eggs Casserole

1 pound asparagus
3 hard boiled eggs
1 tablespoon bread and butter pickles, finely chopped
4 club crackers, crushed
Mayonnaise to moisten eggs
2 tablespoons butter
2 tablespoons flour
1 cup milk
½ cup heavy cream
1 teaspoon salt plus more for asparagus
Nutmeg Paprika
1 cup "Four Cheese Mexican" cheese

Cut boiled eggs in half lengthwise. Remove yolk and place in a bowl with the pickles, crushed crackers, and enough mayonnaise to moisten well. Stuff the eggs. Refrigerate until ready to use.

Remove the woody stem from the asparagus. Wash asparagus to remove any sand or grit. Cut the asparagus into 1- inch pieces. Place the asparagus in a small skillet and cover with water. Cook on high for 5 minutes from the time you set on the skillet on the stove. Remove the asparagus from the water and set aside. In a medium skillet, melt butter and add flour. Cook for 2-3 minutes to cook flour. Do not brown. Whisk in milk and cream. Add salt to taste and a pinch of nutmeg. Cook until slightly thickened.

Sprinkle the asparagus with ¼ teaspoon salt. Place asparagus in a small casserole dish. Top with the stuffed eggs. Pour the sauce over the eggs and asparagus. Top with cheese and sprinkle with paprika. Bake in a 350° oven for 20-25 minutes.

Note: This casserole can be refrigerated until ready to bake. Cook for 35 minutes if refrigerated before baking.

Asparagus Casserole

Sally Rose was one of my personal chef clients and she liked this recipe for asparagus casserole.

1 can asparagus drained and liquid reserved
1 can cream of mushroom soup
4 hard boiled eggs, sliced
¾ pound cheddar cheese
12 saltine or cheese crackers
¾ cup milk

Crumble 4 crackers in bottom of a buttered casserole dish. Place a layer of cheese, eggs, asparagus and soup, then another layer of crackers and another layer of each ingredient until all ingredients except milk are used. Pour milk and 2 teaspoons asparagus juice over the casserole. Sprinkle with the remaining 4 crackers. Bake at 350º for 25-30 minutes.

Asparagus with Sunshine Sauce

My mother made this recipe for many years. My stepfather, John now makes it quite often these days. It's a family favorite.

1-½ pounds fresh asparagus*
¼ cup sauterne or other dry white wine
1 tablespoon instant minced onion
1 tablespoon lemon juice
¾ cup mayonnaise
2 hard-cooked eggs, chopped

*If using fresh asparagus prepare and cook the asparagus.
In a small saucepan, pour wine over onion. Sir in lemon juice and mayonnaise: heat just to boiling. Gently stir in eggs. Serve hot over spears. 4 to 6 servings

Roasted Asparagus

1 pound asparagus spears
1 tablespoon olive oil
Salt, pepper
Lemon juice

Preheat oven to 400°. Wash asparagus, and snap off tough ends and discard. Dry the asparagus and place the spears on a baking sheet. Coat with the olive oil. Sprinkle lightly with salt and pepper. Bake for 15 minutes. Remove from the oven and sprinkle lightly with lemon juice. Serves 4.

Asparagus with Hollandaise Sauce

¼ pound or 11 spring asparagus spears per person

Trim the asparagus spears at the woody, tough stem end. Wash the spears to remove any sand. Place the spears in a large skillet and cover with water. Turn the burner to high heat and cook for 7 minutes. Remove from heat.

While asparagus is cooking, prepare hollandaise sauce.

Hollandaise Sauce:

¼ cup butter (1/2 stick)
2 egg yolks, slightly beaten
¼ cup butter, melted (1/2 stick)
1 tablespoon lemon juice
Pinch salt
Cayenne pepper to taste

Put ¼ cup cold butter and egg yolks into the top of a double boiler over medium heat. Do not let water boil. Stir until the butter melts. Very slowly, drizzle in the ¼ cup melted butter, whisking while you pour. Stir until the mixture thickens. Add the lemon juice, salt and cayenne pepper. Note: If the mixture breaks or separates, remove from heat, add an ice cube, put back on the heat and stir until the mixture comes back together again.

Barbecued Green Beans

6 slices bacon diced
1 onion, chopped
4 (16-ounce) cans cut green beans, drained
1 cup brown sugar—firmly packed
1 cup catsup

Cook the bacon and onion together in a medium-size skillet over medium heat until bacon is crisp. Remove bacon and onions with a slotted spoon and place in an ungreased 2 quart baking dish. Add green beans. Add sugar and catsup and fold into green beans. Bake, covered in a pre-heated 250° oven for 3 hours. Serves 6-8.

Green Beans Madeira

I don't remember where I got this recipe, but it's delicious! I love cooking with Madeira, because it gives the food a hint of nuttiness. I passed it along to my friend Cici Goodyear, and now she makes it for her holiday dinners.

2 tablespoons butter
1 (16-ounce) package mushrooms
1 teaspoon dried thyme
2 shallots, finely chopped
½ cup Madeira
1 cup heavy whipping cream
1-1/4 pounds fresh green beans, trimmed
Vegetable oil
2 large shallots cut into thin slices for garnish

Add beans to a small amount of boiling water and cook for 10 minutes or until very tender. Drain. Set aside. (Or steam the beans in a microwave safe dish until tender). Slice mushrooms. Melt butter in a large skillet over medium high heat. Add mushrooms and thyme and sauté for 5 minutes. Add shallots and sauté for 3 minutes. Add Madeira, and cook until liquid evaporates. Add whipping cream, and cook for 3-5 minutes or until slightly thickened. Remove from heat. Spoon into a greased 2 quart gratin dish or shallow baking dish. Add the beans to the mushroom mixture and toss gently. Pour vegetable oil to depth of 2-inches into a deep saucepan. Heat the oil to 350° degrees. Separate the shallot slices and fry them until very lightly golden. Drain. Sprinkle with salt. Sprinkle the shallots over the green bean mixture and bake in a preheated 400°degree oven for 15 minutes or until thoroughly heated.
Note: If shallots start to get too brown after going in the oven, cover with foil to keep them from burning.

My French Green Bean Casserole

I love this green bean casserole. It's not made with soup! It's easy and delicious and can be made with ingredients already in your pantry.

2 (14.5-ounce) cans French style green beans, drained
1 small can French Fried Onion rings
3 tablespoons butter
3 tablespoons flour
1 cup chicken broth
1 cup heavy cream
1 tablespoon brandy (this adds a nutty flavor)
½-1 teaspoon salt
Dash of pepper
Pinch of nutmeg

Preheat the oven to 350º. Butter or spray a medium size casserole dish. A soufflé dish works well for this casserole. In a medium saucepan, melt the butter and add the flour. Stir until flour has cooked but not browned, about 2-3 minutes. Add the cup of chicken broth, and the cup of heavy cream, brandy, salt, and nutmeg. Allow the mixture to thicken. When slightly thickened, remove from heat. Place one can of the green beans in the casserole. Add half the onion rings. Add half the heavy cream mixture. Add the other can of green beans over this mixture. And repeat the onion rings and heavy cream. Bake for about 30-40 minutes until thick and bubbly.

Mama Lo's Broccoli Casserole

My cousin Sonny Howard owned Herlong Mansion in Micanopy, FL. When I lived in the Orlando area I would go up to visit Sonny and we would set out on a quest to find some really good food! We found that place in Mama Lo's, a restaurant in an old house near the campus of UF in Gainesville. One day we went there to eat and Mama Lo, since passed away, was working in her kitchen. She had a pot of chicken and dumplings, but only one helping of collards. Being the southern gentleman that my cousin is, he let me have the collards! We had the most delicious country dinner—or lunch as people call it these days. The check was 2.95 per person. The only recipe that I've been able to get of Mama Lo's is the Broccoli Casserole. I've made it many times.

5 slices day old white bread, torn into bite size pieces
1 bunch broccoli
3 eggs
¼ cup milk
4 tablespoons butter
1 cup grated cheese
1 teaspoon salt
3 tablespoons sugar (use a little less if you like)

Preheat oven to 350º. Butter an 8-inch square glass baking pan. Cover the bottom of the dish generously with the torn bread. Cut broccoli (head and tops of stems) into bite size pieces and lay broccoli on top of bread. Mix together all remaining ingredients. Pour over broccoli and bread. Cover with foil and bake for 35 minutes. Serves 6.

Broccoli, Corn, Cheese Casserole

5 cups chopped broccoli florets
2 tablespoons water
1 (24-ounce) carton cottage cheese
4 eggs
½ stick butter, melted
1/3 cup all-purpose flour
1 (11-ounce) can whole kernel corn, drained
2 cups shredded cheddar cheese
¼ cup finely chopped onion
½ teaspoon salt
¼ teaspoon black pepper
8 slices bacon cooked and crumbled

Place broccoli in a dish, add the 2 tablespoons water. Cover and microwave for 4 minutes or until slightly tender. Drain, and set aside.
Preheat the oven to 350º. Combine cottage cheese, eggs, butter and flour in a food processor or blender. Process until smooth. Set aside.
Combine the broccoli, corn, cheddar cheese, onion, salt and pepper in a large bowl. Stir in cottage cheese mixture. Stir to combine all ingredients well. Pour into a greased (with non-stick spray) 13 x 9-inch casserole. Sprinkle with bacon. Bake for 45 minutes. Makes 8 servings.

Spicy Broccoli

1 large broccoli crown
2 tablespoons olive oil
¼ to ½ teaspoon red pepper flakes

Wash and dry broccoli. Cut the broccoli into 1-inch pieces or florets. Heat the olive oil in a large heavy skillet. When the oil is hot, put in the red pepper. Then add the broccoli and stir constantly until broccoli is tender.

Brussels Sprouts

It's easy to work with frozen Brussels sprouts when you thaw them in the microwave.

1 small bag frozen Brussels sprouts
3 tablespoons butter
½ cup chopped pecans or hazelnuts, toasted

Place the Brussels sprouts in a microwave safe dish. Cook in the microwave until the sprouts are thawed and steaming. Drain if there is any liquid in the container.
Heat butter to sizzling in a skillet. Cook sprouts in the sizzling butter until tender. Add the nuts just before removing from the skillet. Serves 4-6.

Roasted Brussels Sprouts

1 cup fresh Brussels sprouts per person
Olive oil
2 tablespoons toasted pecans per person

Preheat the oven to 400°. Cut off the stem end of the sprout. Pull away any brown or discolored leaves. With a sharp knife, halve the sprouts. Place the sprout halves on a baking sheet and using your hands, coat the sprouts with olive oil. Roast for about 10-15 minutes or until tender and slightly caramelized. When tender remove from the oven and place in a bowl. Toss with the toasted pecans, and salt and pepper.
Serves 4-6.

Layered Cabbage Casserole

Oh gosh this is good! The evaporated milk makes it very rich.

1 medium head cabbage
¼ cup butter
¼ cup all-purpose flour
½ teaspoon salt
¼ teaspoon pepper
2 cups evaporated milk
¼ cup chopped green pepper
¼ cup chopped onion
2/3 cup shredded Cheddar cheese
½ cup mayonnaise
3 tablespoons chili sauce

Preheat the oven to 350°. Cut the cabbage into small thin wedges. Cook in boiling water until tender. Drain and place the cabbage into a 13 x 9-inch dish and set aside. In a small saucepan, melt the butter and stir in the flour, salt and pepper. Gradually stir in milk. Cook over medium heat until thickened, stirring constantly. Pour the sauce over the cabbage. Bake for 20 minutes.
In a mixing bowl, combine the green pepper, onion, cheese, mayonnaise and chili sauce. Mix well. Spoon over the cabbage. Return to the oven and bake for and additional 20 minutes. Serves 8.

Cauliflower-Pecan Casserole

1 cup water
½ teaspoon salt
2 pounds cauliflower, in florets
4 ounces Cheddar cheese
1 cup sour cream
1 tablespoon all-purpose flour
2 teaspoons chicken broth or water
1 teaspoon dry mustard
½ cup chopped pecans
¼ cup bread crumbs
1 tablespoon butter, melted
1 teaspoon dried marjoram
1 small clove garlic, minced

Place the water and salt in a large pan and bring to a boil. Add the cauliflower and let the water come back to a boil. Lower the heat and simmer until the cauliflower is tender. This will take about 10 minutes. Drain the cauliflower and place in a buttered baking dish.

Preheat the oven to 400º. Mix the Cheddar cheese, sour cream, flour, chicken broth, and mustard together. Pour over the cauliflower. Toss the pecans and bread crumbs with the butter, marjoram, and garlic and sprinkle on top of the cauliflower. Bake until casserole is bubbly and cooked thoroughly. Serves 6-8.

Roasted Cauliflower

One large cauliflower
Olive Oil
Salt and pepper
Marjoram

Preheat oven to 400º. Slice cauliflower into 3/4-inch thick slices vertically down the top of the cauliflower. Rub both sides of each slice with olive oil, salt and pepper. Sprinkle lightly with marjoram. Bake about 15 minutes, turning half way through cooking until caramelized and tender.

Butterbean Casserole

2 (10-ounce) packages frozen butter beans or baby lima beans cooked in 2 cups water
5 slices maple flavored bacon, or ½ cup country ham
¼ cup chopped green onions
2 tablespoons flour
3 tablespoons light brown sugar
1-1/2 tablespoons dry mustard
1-1/2 tablespoons fresh lemon juice
1-1/2 teaspoons salt
¼ teaspoon pepper

Topping:
¾ cup bread crumbs
3 tablespoons butter

Cook butter beans in the 2 cups water until very tender, about 25 minutes. Add more liquid if beans become too dry. Drain the limas and reserve 1 cup of liquid from the beans. Fry bacon in a large skillet until crisp. Remove bacon and set aside. Sauté green onions in bacon fat. Add the flour to the bacon drippings, and green onions and whisk, stirring until flour is smooth. Cook for 1-2 minutes to cook the flour. Gradually add the 1 cup of bean liquid, whisking until smooth. Cook until the mixture is thickened. Stir in the brown sugar, mustard, lemon juice, salt and pepper. (If mixture becomes too thick, add more liquid.) Place the beans in a casserole dish and pour the sauce over them. Melt butter and mix with bread crumbs and place on top of casserole. Crumble bacon over the crumb mixture. Bake in a 350º oven for 20-25 minutes or until bubbly.
*Note: Use Country Ham instead of bacon for a different flavor.

My Cousin Sue Belle Rogers Smith's English Pea Casserole

I was very fond of my cousin Sue who passed away a few years ago. Sue passed along some of her recipes before she died. Sue lived her entire life in Sweet Water, Alabama. She was a good and sweet person.

1 (16-ounce) can tiny English peas with Onions and Mushrooms, half the liquid drained
1 can cream of mushroom soup
1 tablespoon flour
Grated Cheddar cheese
3 hard boiled eggs, sliced
1 small jar diced pimiento, drained
Buttery cracker crumbs

Combine all ingredients except the cracker crumbs and cheese. Line the bottom of a small casserole dish with cracker crumbs. Pour in the pea and mushroom mixture. Add enough cracker crumbs and cheese to cover the top of the casserole. Bake in a preheated 350º oven for 25-30 minutes until bubbly and slightly golden brown on top. Serve 4-6.

Summer Corn

12 ears fresh white sweet corn
4 tablespoons Butter or bacon fat
Heavy cream or milk
Salt and pepper to taste

Shuck the corn and remove any silks. Cut the corn from the cob into a bowl. Using a spoon, scrape the cob to remove any milk and let it fall into the bowl of corn. Melt the butter in a large skillet. Add the corn. Bring to a simmer and let the corn cook, stirring frequently so that it does not burn. Add a small amount of water if needed to make it more liquid. When the corn has reached the tenderness that you want, add the salt and pepper and about ½ cup or more of heavy cream. Let the corn and cream cook together for 1-2 minutes. Add more cream if needed. Taste for seasoning.

Southern Corn Casserole

2 (15-ounce) cans cream style corn
2 tablespoons sugar
1 teaspoon salt
3 tablespoons butter
5 eggs, beaten
1 cup milk
1 tablespoon cornstarch
1 tablespoon cold water

Preheat the oven to 350º. Mix corn, sugar, salt, butter, eggs and milk. Add cornstarch to water and then mix with the corn mixture. Pour into a greased, shallow 2 quart baking dish. Bake for 1 hour or until corn mixture set. Serves 6.

Corn Pudding

This casserole is made with frozen corn, compared to the one above that is made with canned corn. You can use this recipe in the summer with fresh corn.

10-12 ears white corn or 2 (10-ounce) boxes frozen white corn
¼ cup all-purpose flour
1 tablespoon sugar
1 teaspoon salt
¼ teaspoon pepper
3-4 dashes cayenne pepper
2 cups light coffee cream or 2 cups half and half
½ stick butter, melted
3 eggs well-beaten

Cut corn from ears. If using frozen corn, thaw and drain in a colander. Puree ½ the corn in a blender for 5 seconds. Combine pureed corn with whole corn in a large bowl. Add the flour, sugar, eggs, salt, pepper, cayenne pepper, melted butter and cream. Pour into a 1-1/2 quart casserole that has been sprayed with a non-stick cooking spray. Put the casserole dish in a hot water bath with the water depth at about 1-inch. Bake in a 350º oven for about an hour and 10 minutes or until corn is set and a knife blade inserted in the center comes out clean.

Creole Corn

6 slices bacon
3 tablespoons flour
1 (11-ounce) can shoe peg corn, drained
1 (14.5 ounce) can diced tomatoes, undrained
1 small onion, finely chopped
1 stalk celery, finely chopped
4 ounces grated cheese
¼ teaspoon salt
1/8 teaspoon pepper

Cook the bacon in a heavy skillet. Remove from the skillet when brown and crisp and set aside. Add the flour to the bacon drippings and cook until flour is browned. Add the corn, tomatoes, celery, onion, salt and pepper. Mix well and remove from the heat. Make 2 layers in an oven proof casserole dish, alternating vegetables and grated cheese. Cover and bake for 30 minutes in a pre-heated 350°oven. Serves 8.

Good Old Collard Greens

I like my collards well-done. If you like yours a little crisp just don't cook them as long.

8 slices bacon, chopped
1 large onion, finely chopped
1 (14.5-ounce) can chicken broth
2 tablespoon apple cider vinegar
2 tablespoon brown sugar, firmly packed
½ teaspoon dried hot red pepper flakes
4 pounds collards

Remove ribs and stems from collards. Wash collards in three waters. Wash drain, wash drain, wash drain. Cut the collards in a chiffonade. A chiffonade is when several collard leaves are stacked on each other, rolled and then sliced. Leave the collards wet from the washing, and slice the collards about 1/2-inch wide. Set aside. In a Dutch oven, cook bacon until crisp. Remove the bacon and set aside. Add onions to the bacon drippings and cook until caramelized or until slightly browned. Add collards to the onion mixture while collards are still slightly wet. Cover and cook down, stirring occasionally so that the collards don't burn. When the liquid has cooked out, gradually add the broth as needed to moisten. When collards are tender add the remaining ingredients into the collards. Sprinkle the bacon on top before serving. Serves 8.

Eggplant Parmesan

1 small eggplant
1 cup seasoned bread crumbs*
Oil for frying
1 (14.5-ounce) can Italian style diced tomatoes
1 small package mozzarella cheese
1 teaspoon sugar

Peel the eggplant and cut into slices about ½-inch thick. Salt the eggplant on both sides. Let the eggplant sit on paper towels for about 15 minutes, then dip the eggplant in seasoned bread crumbs, and fry in vegetable oil until tender. Put about ¼ of the tomatoes into the bottom of a buttered or sprayed 8 x 8-inch baking dish, or 9-inch pie pan. Place the eggplant on top of the tomatoes. Sprinkle with ½ the cheese. Pour remaining tomatoes over the eggplant, and sprinkle with the sugar then the remaining cheese. Bake at 350º for 25-30 minutes.
*If you would like to dip the eggplant in an egg wash, dip in flour to hold the egg wash, then dip in egg and then in seasoned bread crumbs.

Eggplant Pie

1 stick unsalted butter
1 medium eggplant, peeled and cubed (about 4 cups)
2 cups coarsely chopped fresh mushrooms
2 cloves garlic, minced
4 tablespoons chopped fresh parsley
1 teaspoon salt
½ cup tomato paste
1 (9-inch) pastry shell, unbaked
¼ cup freshly grated parmesan

Preheat the oven to 350º. Melt the butter in a large skillet and sauté the eggplant over medium-high heat. Cover and cook for 10 minutes over low heat. Add the mushrooms and garlic and cook, stirring constantly until mushrooms begin to wilt. Add parsley, salt and tomato paste. Stir until blended. Spoon the mixture into the pastry shell. Bake for 45 minutes. Cool slightly before serving. Sprinkle with Parmesan. Serves 4.

Leeks Au Gratin

12 leeks
¾ cup heavy whipping cream
3 cups white Cheddar cheese
Seasoned bread crumbs (see seasoning below)

Leeks: Remove the root end and the green end of the leek and use the white part only. Cut the leeks down the center and cut into 1-inch lengths. Wash the leeks to remove any sand or dirt. Drain. Place the leeks in an 11 x 7-inch baking dish or if making a thin layer use a 13 x 9-inch baking dish. Cover with plastic wrap and microwave for 8-10 minutes or until leeks are cooked. Remove the plastic cover. Cool the leeks. (If you need to bake right away, place the leeks in another dish to microwave and then place in the baking dish.) Add the cream and sprinkle with salt and pepper. Sprinkle the cheese over the cream. Bake in a preheated 350º oven for 15-20 minutes or until hot and bubbly in the center. Remove from the oven and add the bread crumbs and cook for another 5-8 minutes.
Seasoning: 6 slices of a French baguette placed in a food processor and processed to crumbs. Add 1 teaspoon dried parsley, ¼ teaspoon dried basil and ¼ teaspoon marjoram. Mix crumbs and herbs together.

Mushrooms in Cream

24 large mushroom caps
½ cup butter, softened
2 small shallots, minced
3 tablespoons chopped fresh parsley
1-1/2 teaspoons chopped chives
Salt to taste
½ teaspoon lemon juice
1 cup heavy cream

Remove the stems from the mushroom caps and save for another use, or discard. Stuff the caps with butter, shallots, parsley, salt and lemon juice. Put the mushroom caps in a single layer in an oven proof baking dish. Pour the heavy cream over the mushrooms. Bake in a 450ºoven for 10 minutes. Serve hot. Serves 8.

Pineapple Casserole

This recipe is from my friend Nell Redfern of Gilmer, TX. I've made this many times and it always hits the spot.

1 (20-ounce) can pineapple chunks or tidbits
½ cup sugar
4 tablespoons butter, melted
3 tablespoons flour
1 cup grated Cheddar cheese
½ cup crushed buttery crackers

Drain the pineapple and reserve 3 tablespoons of the juice. Combine sugar, flour and juice. Mix well. Add the pineapple and cheese. Mix the butter and the crackers. Place the pineapple mixture in an oven proof casserole. Place the buttered crumbs on top.
Bake in a preheated 350º oven for 25 minutes.

Spinach Bake

Mother's recipe!

2 eggs beaten
¾ cup mayonnaise, divided
2 (10-ounce) packages chopped frozen spinach, thawed and well-drained
1 (14-ounce) can artichoke hearts, drained and cut into quarters
½ cup sour cream
¼ cup freshly grated Parmesan cheese
6 bacon slices, cooked crisp

Combine eggs, ½ cup of the mayonnaise, and mix until well blended. Add the spinach and artichoke hearts. Spoon mixture into a lightly greased 10 x 6-inch baking dish. Combine the remaining mayonnaise, sour cream and cheese mixing well. Spoon over the spinach mixture. Bake in a preheated 350º oven for 30 minutes or until set. Sprinkle with bacon before serving. Serves 8.

Spinach Parmesan

I love creamed spinach with cheese so this fills the bill! You can change the cheese to Gruyere or grated Swiss or any cheese that you like.

6 (10-ounce) packages frozen chopped spinach
2 cups freshly grated Parmesan or grated Gruyere
½ cup finely chopped onion
2/3 cup heavy cream
½ stick butter, melted
1 heavy dash grated nutmeg
½ teaspoon salt

Preheat oven to 350º. Cook and drain spinach. Squeeze the spinach to remove any excess moisture. Place the spinach in a large bowl. Add the remaining ingredients. Pour the mixture into a buttered 13 x 9-inch baking dish. Bake at 350° for 25-30 minutes or until bubbly in the center. May be made ahead and frozen.

Delicious Squash Casserole

My Aunt Elizabeth Henderson makes the most delicious squash. Aunt"Sis" lives in Hattiesburg, Mississippi. I've always thought she was a great cook, so when I decided that I was tired of the same old squash recipe, I turned to Mississippi for a good old Southern recipe. I love this squash casserole recipe and so does everyone else that has it!

3 pounds of yellow crookneck squash
Salt and pepper
1 small onion, finely chopped
1 small green pepper, finely chopped
1 cup freshly grated Parmesan cheese or Cheddar cheese
¾ cup mayonnaise
2 eggs, beaten

Slice squash into ½ inch rounds and cook covered in water seasoned with salt and pepper, until squash is tender when pierced with a fork, about 20 minutes. Drain well. Combine squash and remaining ingredients and pour into a greased casserole. Bake at 350º for 40-45 minutes.

Anderson Squash Casserole

This recipe came from one of my personal chef clients in Anderson, SC.
I really enjoy the flavor that Greek seasoning adds to this casserole
This recipe will make you want to eat squash more often.

2 pounds small yellow squash
1 small onion, chopped
2/3 cup chopped bell pepper
2 ounces Swiss cheese, cubed
1 (2-ounce) jar diced pimiento, drained
Greek seasoning
1 egg, slightly beaten
1 tablespoon mayonnaise
1 can French fried onion rings
Salt to taste
Pepper to taste

Wash and thinly slice wet squash. Layer with onions, and sprinkle each layer with Greek seasoning, salt and pepper. Cook on high heat. Stir so that squash browns slightly but does not burn. When the squash is done, remove the lid and allow the liquid to evaporate. Mash the squash. Add the mayonnaise, cheese, bell pepper, and pimiento. Pour the squash into a 1-1/2 quart casserole that has been sprayed with cooking spray. Bake in a 350º oven for 20 minutes. Add onion rings to the top and bake for another 10 minutes.

Tomato Pie

I was on a mini-vacation in Portland, Maine. As usual, I was wandering through a used book store looking around when I came across a "1955 Congressional Record Cookbook." I was so surprised to find tomato pie in the book. It was a little different from the tomato pie that we make today with ready-made piecrust, because the pie in 1955 had a biscuit crust, and didn't have basil. All the recipes in the book were hand-written. I was just fascinated by this book, so I bought it. What a treasure it is. I have found so many recipes in the book that I thought were fairly new, but cooks were making them before 1955!

1 pre-baked 9 inch pie crust
1-1/2 to 2 ripe tomatoes, peeled
1 tablespoon dried basil or 3 tablespoons fresh basil, chopped
1 small to medium sweet onion, finely chopped
1 ½ cups grated sharp Cheddar cheese
¾-1 cup mayonnaise
Salt and pepper to taste

Blind bake the pie crust according to package direction.
Peel tomatoes, slice into ½-3/4 inch slices and set aside to drain.
Place tomatoes in the pie shell in ONE layer, top with chopped onion and salt and pepper to taste. Sprinkle with basil.
Mix cheese and mayonnaise and spread over the onions to make a top crust from edge to edge of the piecrust. Bake at 350º for 30-35 minutes. Top will be bubbly when pie is ready. Wait 20 minutes before serving.
*Small tomato pies can be made in tart pans using the same method as above. These are great for tea parties.

Italian Baked Tomatoes

Great with steak!

1 tomato per person
Zesty Italian Salad Dressing
Freshly grated Parmesan Cheese

Cut tomatoes in half. Pierce the tomato halves with a fork. Sprinkle with Italian Dressing.
Place the tomatoes on a foil lined baking pan, or an oven proof baking dish. Bake in a preheated 350°
oven until tomatoes are tender. Sprinkle with grated parmesan. Serve hot.

Sautéed Tomatoes

1 container grape tomatoes
2 tablespoons butter
Salt and pepper to taste
Favorite herbs such as thyme or basil

Melt butter in skillet until sizzling. Add grape tomatoes. Sauté until tender. Salt and pepper to taste.
Add fresh herbs just before removing from heat. Serve hot.

Fried Ripe Tomatoes (1)

4 firm, ripe tomatoes, sliced to about ¾ inch thickness
2 eggs
Seasoned flour or cracker meal
½ or more teaspoon salt
¼ or more teaspoon pepper
Olive oil

Sprinkle tomato slices with salt and pepper. Dip tomato slices in beaten egg. And then dip in seasoned flour or cracker meal. Cook in hot oil until tomatoes are golden brown on both sides. Serve hot. Serve with cream gravy for breakfast, lunch or supper.

Fried Red Tomatoes (2)

4 large, firm red ripe tomatoes
1 cup flour
½ teaspoon brown sugar
½ teaspoon salt
¼ teaspoon pepper
2 tablespoon butter
2 tablespoons olive oil

Slice tomatoes about ¾-inch thick. Mix sugar, salt, pepper and flour together. Dip sliced tomatoes in the flour mixture to coat. Melt butter in a large skillet and add olive oil. When butter and oil are sizzling add tomato slices. Cook on each side until brown. Remove to a plate in a warm oven until all slices are cooked.

Pasta, Rice & Potatoes

Personal Chef Macaroni & Cheese

1 (8-ounce) box macaroni
4 cups shredded sharp Cheddar or cheese of your choice
1-1/4 cups buttermilk
¾ cup mayonnaise
1 cup cheese crackers, crumbled

Cook macaroni according to package directions. Drain. While the macaroni is still hot add the buttermilk, cheese, and mayonnaise. Pour the mixture into a sprayed 11 x 7-inch casserole dish. Bake at 350º for 20-30 minutes or until hot and bubbly. 6 Servings, maybe!

Smoky Cheese & Rigatoni

I developed this recipe for a cheese company and it appeared in their national magazine last January. Thought I would share it with you.

1 (8-ounce) container rigatoni, cooked according to package directions, and drained
4 tablespoon butter
4 tablespoons flour
1 teaspoon minced garlic
1 cup buttermilk
1 cup milk
¾ pound smoked processed cheese, grated
1 teaspoon country Dijon mustard
1/8 teaspoon grated nutmeg
Salt and pepper to taste
7 cherry tomatoes cut in half

Topping:
3 tablespoons butter, melted
¾ cup bread crumbs
½ cup Romano cheese

Preheat the oven to 350º. In a medium saucepan melt the butter with the garlic. Add the flour and cook for 2-3 minutes to cook the flour. Gradually add the milk and buttermilk, whisking while adding. Add the grated cheese, mustard and nutmeg. Check for seasoning. Add the cherry tomato halves. Add the cheese mixture to the drained pasta and place in an 11 x 7-inch casserole dish that has been sprayed with a non-stick cooking spray.
For the topping; mix the butter, bread crumbs, and Romano cheese. Sprinkle on top of the casserole. Bake at 350º until casserole is hot and bubbly and topping is lightly browned.

Roasted Polenta

This recipe came from Michael Chiarella when I had lessons from him years ago at The Greenbrier. I've changed the recipe a tiny bit! Try this with the Salmon & Sun-dried tomato pesto. If I use it with the salmon, then I don't roast it, but just serve it hot after it has cooked in the heavy pot. Delicious!

3 cups chicken stock
3 cups heavy cream
Pinch nutmeg
¼ teaspoon pepper
1 teaspoon salt
2 cups Quaker yellow cornmeal
1-1/2 cups grated parmesan
2 tablespoons butter

Combine the stock and cream, grated nutmeg, salt and pepper in a large heavy pot. Bring the liquid to a boil. Add the cornmeal gradually and start whisking.
Continue to cook over medium heat while stirring constantly. It will start to get stiff. Stir until the polenta pulls away from the sides of the pot. This should take about 10 minutes. Remove from the heat and add the cheese and butter.
Mix until well incorporated.
Spread the polenta evenly to a depth of about 3/4-inch on oiled baking sheets.
At this point you can freeze if wrapped well, or just cover with parchment paper and refrigerate. Before serving, preheat the oven to 500º. Cut the polenta into squares or triangles. Put on a buttered baking sheet, and sprinkle generously with leftover parmesan cheese. Bake until golden brown.
Note: If you want to serve without roasting, just serve hot and do not roast.

Easy Everyday Polenta

4 cups milk
1 cup yellow cornmeal
1 teaspoon salt
1-1/2 cups grated parmesan cheese
4 tablespoons butter

Bring the milk and salt to a boil. Add cornmeal while whisking. Reduce heat to medium. Stir constantly while cornmeal is thickening. When the mixture starts to pull away from the sides, add the cheese and the butter. Stir to mix all ingredients. Put in a bowl and serve with your favorite pasta sauce.

Oven-dried Tomatoes (see index) and Pasta

Toss oven-dried tomatoes with your favorite pasta, olive oil and basil.

Penne with Goat Cheese, Walnuts, and Green Onions

1 (16-ounce) package penne
1 cup chopped green onions
1 cup chopped walnuts
¼ cup olive oil
4 ounces goat cheese, crumbles
1 cup heavy cream
½ cup freshly grated Pecorino Romano
Freshly ground pepper
Salt to taste

Cook the penne according to package directions. Drain and set aside.
Place the olive oil into a large skillet and sauté the walnuts and green onions over medium-high heat, stirring constantly until the onions are tender. Add the penne and goat cheese. Cook, stirring constantly until the cheese has melted. Remove from the heat and stir in the heavy cream, and cheese. Add salt and pepper to taste. Serves 6.

Potatoes Dauphinois or Classic Potatoes Au Gratin

Classis French cooking! Yum. Potatoes cooked in cream and cheese. How much better can you get?

2 pounds potatoes peeled and thinly sliced
1 cup of finely diced onion
½ pound of grated gruyere or Cheddar cheese
3/4 cup heavy cream
Salt and pepper
Butter

Preheat the oven to 375º. Butter an oven proof baking dish. Place a layer of potato slices on bottom of dish, sprinkle with salt and pepper and dot potatoes on top with butter. Sprinkle the potatoes with onion and cheese. Pour on 2 tablespoons cream. Repeat layers, ending with a layer of cheese. Pour on any remaining cream.
Cover and bake for 1 to 1-1/2 hours or until potatoes are tender. When done, broil the top to brown. Serves 4-6.

Aunt Betty's Potatoes Au Gratin

Betty was a wonderful cook. She always had good food when we visited.

8 medium peeled potatoes
1 large onion, finely chopped
½ cup bell pepper
6 tablespoons butter
6 tablespoons flour
3 cups milk
1-1/2 cups grated Gruyere or Cheddar
Salt and pepper to taste
1 cup additional cheese
Chopped parsley
Paprika

Boil potatoes and set aside to cool. When cooled, slice the potatoes. In a Dutch oven or large pan, melt the butter. Sauté the onion and green pepper until tender. Add the flour and cook for 2-3 minutes. Add the milk and cook until the sauce starts to thicken. Add the cheese and parsley and stir to melt the cheese. Place the sliced potatoes in a large oven-proof casserole dish. Pour the sauce over the potatoes, and sprinkle with additional cheese and paprika. Bake in a preheated 350º oven until bubbly and slightly browned on top.

Mashed Potatoes & Green Onions

4 large russet potatoes, peeled and thinly sliced
½ cup milk or half and half
4 tablespoons unsalted butter
1 tablespoons unsalted butter to sauté onions
2 bunches green onions, chopped
Salt and pepper to taste

Boil potatoes until tender. Drain well and mash or rice until smooth. Blend in milk and butter. Melt 1 tablespoon butter, and add chopped green onions. Sauté onions until tender. Add to potatoes and mix gently. Season with salt and pepper. To keep potatoes warm before serving, place in a heat proof bowl over a pan of hot water. Cover. Serves 4-6.

Roasted Baby Yukon's

3-4 baby Yukon Gold potatoes per person
Olive oil
Rosemary or thyme sprigs

Wash and dry potatoes. Cut in half if too large. Place on a baking sheet and rub with olive oil. Place rosemary or thyme sprigs on potatoes. Roast in a pre-heated 400°oven until potatoes are tender. Great served with chorizo and peppers.

Greek Lemon Roasted Potatoes

8 medium baking potatoes, peeled and quartered
1 cup water
½ cup olive oil
Juice of 3 lemons or about ½ cup
1 tablespoon fresh Greek oregano, finely chopped
2 tablespoons salt or to taste
½ teaspoon freshly ground pepper

Heat oven to 475º. Place potatoes in a heavy metal roasting pan in a single layer. Add the 1-cup water, olive oil, lemon juice, oregano, salt and pepper. Toss potatoes until well coated. Bake uncovered until tender and starting to brown around the edges. Turn potatoes half way through cooking. Serve the potatoes on a large platter with fresh oregano sprigs and lemon wedges. Serve with pork tenderloin with sun-dried tomatoes and balsamic sauce. Serves 8.

Phyllo Potatoes

6 large baking potatoes
6 strips bacon
1 cup sour cream
1 medium onion, finely diced
1 small bunch green onions, including greens, finely chopped
1 teaspoon Maggi seasoning
1 tablespoon all-purpose seasoning (herbs mixed with salt)
Salt and pepper to taste
4 tablespoons butter, cut into chunks
1 (1 pound) box phyllo dough
1 stick butter, melted

Bake potatoes until done. Set aside and keep warm. Finely dice bacon and fry until crisp. Drain well, saving 1 tablespoon bacon drippings. Cut cooked potatoes in half and scoop the potatoes from the shells into a large mixing bowl. Mash the potatoes until mostly smooth. Stir in the sour cream, onions, bacon, reserved 1 tablespoon of bacon drippings, Maggi and all-purpose seasoning. Add the 4 tablespoons of butter in chunks. Mix well. Check for seasoning and add more salt and pepper if needed.
Spray a 13 x 8-inch baking dish with a non-stick cooking spray. Keep phyllo dough soft by unfolding and placing a damp towel on top.
Place a sheet of phyllo on the bottom of the pan. Brush with butter. Keep layering until you have placed and buttered 10 sheets of phyllo. Spread the layered phyllo with the seasoned potato mixture. Begin to layer and butter another 10 more sheets of phyllo on top of the potatoes. Bake in a pre-heated 350° for 25-30 minutes or until the phyllo is golden brown. Cut into squares and serve.

Pam's Swedish Potatoes

Pam's mother made these every holiday when Pam was a child. Pam makes them for her family now. They are delicious!

3 (12-ounce) packages frozen hash brown potatoes (thawed)
2 medium onions, grated or finely chopped
2 cups grated Cheddar cheese
1 can cream of chicken soup
1-1/2 cups sour cream
¼ cup melted butter
Salt and pepper to taste
Enough corn flake crumbs to cover the top
Additional melted butter

Mix all ingredients except corn flake crumbs and additional butter and place in a 13 x 9-inch casserole allowing 1-inch at the top for bubbling over. Top with crushed corn flake crumbs mixed with a little melted butter.
Bake for 1 hour at 350º.

Potato Latkes with Applesauce and Sour Cream

I've had this recipe for years. It really is not as difficult as it looks. So, give it a try.

1 pound baking potatoes
3 large eggs, beaten
¼ cup matzo meal
¼ cup finely chopped onions
¼ teaspoon salt
¼ teaspoon pepper
¼ cup or more of cooking oil
Applesauce
Sour cream

Peel and coarsely shred potatoes. (I use the shredder in my food processor for this). Put the potatoes in cold water until all are shredded to prevent them from turning black. Remove from the cold water and drain. Using a dish towel, wring out the potatoes to remove all of the water.
Add the potatoes to a mixing bowl, stir in the eggs, matzo meal, onion, salt and pepper.
Heat the oil and drop in the latkes 2 tablespoons at a time. Cook until crisp and brown. Drain on paper towels. Serve hot with sour cream and applesauce on the side. Makes about 12 latkes.

Sweet Potato Casserole

My daughter-in-law Pam gave me this recipe. Pam's mother, Pat has made this recipe as long as Pam can remember. I think that Pat got the recipe from her mother.

Casserole:
3 sweet potatoes baked at 400º for 45-60 minutes (you will need 3 cups)
½ cup sugar
2 eggs
1 teaspoon vanilla
½ cup butter, melted

Topping:
½ cup brown sugar
1/3 cup self-rising flour
1 cup nuts
1/3 cup butter (not melted)

Mash the potatoes, and use 3 cups of the potatoes. Add the next 4 ingredients. Pour into a casserole dish. Mix the topping to a crumb consistency. Sprinkle on the casserole and bake in a 350º oven for 30 minutes.

Candied Sweet Potatoes

Another good recipe from Janice Rogers's. There is no liquid for the potatoes to cook in so they caramelize. Very good!

4 cups cubed sweet potatoes
½ cup white sugar
½ cup light brown sugar
1 stick butter
Pinch salt

Place sweet potatoes in a saucepan and cook on very low heat until sweet potatoes are done.

Richard's Charleston Red Rice

Richard is Down's syndrome. He's a great cook. He makes the best red rice, and cornbread. This is Richard's Charleston Red Rice Recipe. And, wow it is good!!! His cornbread recipe is located in the bread section of this cookbook.

2 tablespoons butter
1 onion, chopped
1 stalk celery, chopped
1 cup chopped bell pepper
1 cup rice
1 (14-ounce) package smoked sausage, sliced thin
¾ cup water
½-1 teaspoon salt or to taste
1 (14.5 ounce) can petite diced tomatoes plus a tiny pinch of sugar if the tomatoes are acidic

Richard makes his red rice in a heavy Dutch oven. He melts the butter, adds the chopped onion, celery and bell pepper and cooks them until tender. Then he adds the rice, sausage, tomatoes, water, salt, and pinch sugar. Bring to a boil and reduce to low, cover tightly until the rice is done about 25-30 minutes.

Lavender Rice Pilaf with Hazelnuts

2 tablespoons butter
1 cup long grain rice
2 cups chicken stock
1 (3-inch) stem of lavender
½-1 teaspoon salt
½ cup toasted hazelnuts

Melt butter in a saucepan. Add rice. Stir the rice in the butter for about 5 minutes or until it starts to become golden. Add the chicken stock and the lavender. Season to taste with salt. Bring to a boil, and then reduce heat to a very low simmer. Cover. Cook for 25-30 minutes. Add hazelnuts just before serving.

Rice & Cheese Stuffed Onions

8 yellow onions, about 4 ounces each
½ stick unsalted butter
Salt
1/3 cup raw long grain rice
1-2/3 cups chicken broth
1 sprig lavender if available or ½ teaspoon Herbs of Provence
2 tablespoons grated Swiss or Gruyere cheese
4 tablespoons freshly grated Parmesan cheese
Fresh pepper

Peel the onions, and then cut a very thin slice from the bottom of each one. With a sharp knife cut a wide cone shape from the top of each onion, reserving the centers. Blanch the onion cases in a large pot of boiling, salted water until crisp tender, about 7 minutes. Drain in a colander under cold running water to stop the cooking process. Drain well, placing hollow side down.

Chop the onions centers. Melt 2 tablespoons of the butter in a skillet over medium heat. Add 1-1/2 cups of the chopped onion, sprinkle lightly with salt and sauté, tossing occasionally until soft and lightly golden, about 20 minutes. Add the lavender or Herbs of Provence. Add the rice and stir for 2 minutes. Add 1 cup of the chicken broth and bring to a boil. Lower the heat, cover tightly, and simmer until the rice is tender. This will take about 20-30 minutes. Remove from the heat. Remove the lavender sprig and discard.

Stir the Swiss cheese and 2 tablespoons of the Parmesan into the rice. Season with salt and pepper to taste.

Spoon the filling into the onion shells, mounding up slightly, and place them in a shallow baking dish. Sprinkle the filling with the remaining 2 tablespoons Parmesan. Place the remaining 2 tablespoons butter and 2/3 cup chicken broth around the onions in the baking dish. Spray a piece of foil with cooking spray and cover the onions tent style. Bake in a preheated 350º oven for 25 minutes. Remove the foil and bake until onions are golden, about 20 minutes longer, basting frequently with the broth and butter in bottom of pan.

Mexican Rice Casserole

Mother's recipe.

3 cups cooked rice
1-1/2 cups shredded Mexican cheese or Jack cheese
1 (16-ounce) can cream style corn
2/3 cup sour cream
1 bunch green onions, thinly sliced
1 (4-ounce) can green chilies
2 tablespoons minced cilantro or parsley
½ teaspoon salt
1/8 teaspoon cayenne pepper

Preheat the oven to 375°. In a large bowl mix all ingredients. Place the mixture into a 1-1/2 quart oven-proof casserole dish that has been sprayed with non-stick cooking spray. Bake the casserole uncovered for 35-40 minutes or until golden. Serves 4.

Mother's Yellow Rice

1 package yellow rice
1 can Mexicorn
½ stick butter
1 can cream of celery soup
1 cup shredded Cheddar

Prepare rice according to package directions. Melt butter and mix with rice, corn and soup. Pour into an oiled casserole. Sprinkle the cheese on top of the casserole. Bake at 350° for 25 minutes, or until heated through.

Beef

St. Patrick's Day

March already! Still just enough chill in the air to enjoy the good old comfort food that St. Patrick's Day brings us each year. I've got a classic recipe to make your St. Patrick's Day the best so far.

Like most countries, Ireland has become a diverse society. As we know in this country, along with diversity comes change. And, I wanted to see what changes had been made in the more traditional Irish food for St. Patrick's Day. So, I decided to write to Rory O'Connell, Executive Chef of Ballymaloe House in Cork. Chef O'Connell's response is as follows:

"Dear Linda,"

"There is not a "typical" St. Patrick's Day menu as such, so we tend to serve some of our traditional Irish dishes. The usual dishes that come to mind are Irish Stew, Corned Beef, Carrageen Moss Pudding, Champ, Bacon, and Cabbage, Apple Tart or Cake. We tend to put a great deal of emphasis on the source and quality of ingredients for all our dishes, naming the growers and producers to emphasize the freshness and locality of the produce. My sister's book, The Traditional Food of Ireland by Darina Allen is the masterpiece for this sort of food. I hope this is of some help."

"Kind Regards

Rory O'Connell"

I decided to try Rory's sister's Irish recipe for Corned Beef & Cabbage, and I have to admit that it is the best I've had in my lifetime. It was also the easiest recipe for Corned Beef & Cabbage that I've ever used. Everyone who ate it raved over how good it was. There was not a bite left. It's no surprise since Rory' sister is Darina Allen, famous for her cooking school at Ballymaloe!

Irish Corned Beef & Cabbage

1 (4-pound) corned beef, silverside (if you can find it)
3 large carrots cut into large chunks
6-8 small onions, roughly chopped
1 teaspoon dry English mustard (Coleman's)
Large sprig of fresh thyme, and parsley stalks tied together
1 large Savoy cabbage if available, otherwise a green cabbage
Salt and pepper to taste

Put corned beef into a large Dutch oven with the carrots, onions, mustard and herbs. Add enough cold water to cover the meat. Bring to a boil and simmer covered for 1 hour. Discard outer leaves of the cabbage. Cut the cabbage in quarters and add to the pot. Cook for another 1-1/2 hours or until the meat and vegetables are tender. Serve the corned beef sliced and surrounded by the vegetables. Serve with champ and Irish soda bread, and English mustard.

Elegant Beef Tenderloin

1 (6-pound) beef tenderloin (trimmed size)
Salt and fresh black pepper
½ cup olive oil
½ cup sherry vinegar
1 clove garlic, chopped

Place tenderloin, olive oil, and sherry vinegar in a plastic bag. Marinate for several hours or overnight. Remove from the bag. Salt and pepper the tenderloin.
Line a roasting pan with foil. Place the tenderloin on a wire rack in the roasting pan. Insert a meat thermometer in the thickest part of the tenderloin. Roast in a preheated 425° oven for 30 minutes or until the internal temperature reaches 140° for rare, 150° for medium rare and 160°for medium. Remove to a cutting board and rest the meat for 10-15 minutes to let the juices settle in the meat. Serve with Madeira Blue Cheese Sauce. (See sauces).

Filet of Beef with Roquefort Sauce

This recipe is one from the late Peter Kump. He owned the Peter Kump Cooking School in New York. He was one of the guest chefs at The Greenbrier. Peter Kump and Julia Child were founders of The James Beard Foundation.

2 pounds center piece beef tenderloin, trimmed to 1-3/4 pounds
Salt and freshly ground pepper
1-2 tablespoons canola oil
1 tablespoon minced shallot
3 tablespoons dry Madeira wine
2 cups meat stock reduced to ½ cup or ½ cup demi-glace
1/3 cup heavy cream
2 ounces Roquefort cheese
4-5 tablespoons unsalted butter
6 tablespoons chopped walnuts
1 tablespoon minced fresh parsley

Lightly sprinkle the meat with salt and pepper. Rub a little oil on the beef and refrigerate, loosely covered with plastic wrap for up to 24 hours. One or two hours before cooking, remove the meat from the refrigerator and pat dry. Heat a heavy non-stick skillet and rub a little more oil all over the fillet, then sear it on all sides, about 4 minutes total; or if using a cast iron frying pan put about two teaspoons of the oil in the pan rather than on the meat and sear as directed. Transfer meat to a wire rack and let rest for at least 20 minutes. Set the pan aside to use again.

Preheat the oven to 350°. Place the nuts on a baking tray and lightly toast, about 10 minutes.

Meanwhile discard any fat in the pan, add the shallots and Madeira to the skillet and reduce to a glaze. Add the stock and reduce to a syrupy consistency, about 10 minutes. Then add the cream and cook until the sauce has a nice beige color.

In a food processor mix the Roquefort and 4 tablespoons of the butter until smooth and creamy. If too salty, add up to another tablespoon of butter. Separate into four parts and refrigerate.

Preheat the oven to 450° for 30 minutes before the final cooking. Finish the beef fillet in the oven, 18 minutes for "black and blue", 19 minutes for rare, 20 minutes for medium rare.

Over a low heat, gently re-warm the syrupy sauce in the skillet. Swirl in the cheese, butter mixture pieces, one by one. Spoon sauce onto a warm serving plate. Slice meat and arrange in overlapping slices on the sauce. Garnish with the toasted walnuts and parsley.

Tavern Beef Stroganoff

I got this recipe for beef stroganoff from The Greenbrier. It has been served there for years and it's quite delicious.

2-1/2 pounds beef tenderloin cut into 2-inch x ½- inch strips
1 teaspoon mild paprika
Salt and freshly ground pepper
6 tablespoons unsalted butter
2 cups thinly sliced mushrooms (5 ounces)
½ cup chopped shallots (3 medium shallots)
3 tablespoons all-purpose flour
¾ cup dry white wine
1 cup veal or beef stock
¾ cup sour cream
½ cup julienne of dill pickle

Sprinkle beef with paprika, salt and pepper, tossing to coat evenly. In a large sauté pan, heat half the butter and sauté the beef over high heat until just browned on the outside but rare on the inside, about 1 minute. (Do this in batches to avoid overcrowding the pan, otherwise you will be steaming the meat and it will be tough). Set the meat aside.
Add the remaining butter to the sauté pan and sauté the mushrooms until all their liquid has been rendered and evaporated, 4-5 minutes. Add the shallots and continue to sauté until they are soft and mushrooms are slightly brown, another 2-3 minutes.
Sprinkle the flour over the mushrooms and stir until mixed. Add the wine, stirring to avoid lumps, and boil for about 1 minute, then add the stock, reduce the heat and simmer until slightly thickened, about 10 minutes. Remove from the heat, stir in the sour cream, and add the meat and any accumulated juices. Return to low heat and cook for a few minutes to warm the meat. (Once the sour cream is added, do not boil or it will curdle). Taste and correct seasonings. Ladle over egg noodles in a large serving platter. Garnish with the dill pickles. Serves 6.

"My Mother's Beef Brisket"

This is not my mother's recipe but one that I found in Gourmet in 1995. I believe it is the recipe of the Editor's mother. But, I can tell you that it's delicious.

1 (5-6 pound) beef brisket
(Salt and pepper for brisket)
3 tablespoon vegetable oil
3 large onions cut into 1/2-inch pieces
2-3 large garlic cloves, minced
1 teaspoon Hungarian paprika
¾ teaspoon salt
¾ teaspoon pepper

Preheat the oven to 375°. In a large Dutch oven or other heavy baking pan large enough to hold the brisket, heat 1 tablespoon oil in the oven for 10 minutes. Pat the brisket dry and season with salt and pepper. Roast the brisket in the pan, uncovered for 30 minutes.
While the brisket is roasting, in a large heavy skillet cook the onions in the remaining 2 tablespoons oil over moderately high heat, stirring until the onions are softened and beginning to turn a golden. Reduce heat to medium and cook the onions stirring occasionally. When deep golden, stir in the paprika, salt and pepper and cook for 1 minute. Stir in 3 cups water and bring to a boil.
Spoon the onion mixture over the brisket and bake, covered with a lid, slightly ajar for 3-1/2 hours or until the brisket is tender. (Check the pan every hour to make sure you have enough liquid, and add more water if necessary). Remove the brisket from the oven and let cool in the onion mixture for one hour.
Remove the brisket from the pan, scraping the onion mixture back into the pan. Chill the brisket wrapped in foil overnight. Spoon the onion mixture into a 1 quart measure and chill, covered overnight.
Preheat the oven to 350°. Discard fat from the onion mixture, and add enough water to mixture to measure 3 cups total. Blend in a blender until smooth. Slice the brisket against the grain as thick or thin as your prefer. In a large oven-proof skillet, heat the "gravy" until hot, add the brisket and heat in the oven for 30 minutes. Serves 8-10.

My Easy Pot Roast

I made this pot roast one day when I was looking for an easy dinner since I was very busy. I just threw it all in the same pot.

1 (3-5 pound) boneless chuck roast (7-blade if available)
1 or 2 package(s) beef-onion soup mix (I use two for a larger roast)
1 cup water
1 (14.5-ounce) can diced tomatoes
10 small whole new potatoes
1 small package frozen carrots

Brown the roast on top of stove in a Dutch oven, in a small amount of oil. Add remaining ingredients. Place in a 325° degree oven and bake for about 3 hours, covered. (Optional: After 2-1/2 hours add 2 tablespoons cornstarch to 2 tablespoons cold water and add it to the pan, and bake an additional 30 minutes.) Salt and pepper to taste.

Veal Rolls with Marinara

4 veal scallops, pounded thin
8 slices provolone or mozzarella
5-6 fresh spinach leaves per veal slice
8 thin slices ham, or country ham
3 tablespoons butter
1 tablespoon olive oil
Freshly grated Parmesan
Your favorite marinara sauce

Place cheese, spinach and ham on top of veal slice. Roll up veal slice and secure with a toothpick. Melt butter and add olive oil to a medium skillet. Brown veal rolls on each side. Remove rolls to an oven proof baking dish. Cover with marinara and grated parmesan. Bake in a 350° oven for about 30-45 minutes, or until veal rolls are cooked through. Serve with some good crusty bread.

Cube Steak Grillades & Creamy Baked Cheese Grits

Jim & Joyce Logan were my friends and my customers in the cooking classes that I held at Judy Booker's store in Anderson, SC. I made this dish for one of the classes they attended. Jim told me later that he had made this at home and substituted beef cube steak for the steak called for in the recipe. I thought, what a good idea, it sure would save the tenderizing process. Joyce passed away this past spring. She is certainly missed. This one is for you Joyce!

6 small single serving cube steaks
1 to 2 teaspoons salt
1 to 2 teaspoons black pepper
1/2 cup oil, divided
5 tablespoons flour
1 large onion, chopped
1 bell pepper, chopped
½ cup chopped green onions
1/4 cup chopped celery
3 garlic cloves, finely chopped
¼ cup chopped fresh parsley
1 teaspoon thyme or two thyme sprigs
1 cup beef broth
1 (14.5-ounce) can stewed tomatoes
2 bay leaves

Salt and pepper both sides of the cube steaks. Heat 5 tablespoons oil to the Dutch oven. Fry steak in hot oil until brown. Take cube steak out and set aside.
Add the remaining oil to drippings in the Dutch oven. Add flour, scraping the pan. Cook over medium heat for 3-5 minutes, stirring constantly. Stir in chopped onions, green peppers, celery, garlic, parsley and thyme. Cook for 5 minutes or until vegetables are tender, stirring constantly. Stir in the beef broth, stewed tomatoes and bay leaves. Add the cube steak back into the liquid and bring to a boil. Cover and reduce the heat. Simmer for 1 to 1-1/2 hours or until beef is tender. Discard bay leaves before serving. Serve over creamy baked cheese grits. Serves 6.

Creamy Baked Cheese Grits

5 cups milk
1 teaspoon salt
1-1/3 cups quick cooking grits, uncooked (not instant)
2 cups shredded sharp Cheddar
¼ teaspoon dried thyme
4 tablespoons butter
½ cup grated parmesan cheese

Bring milk, thyme and salt to a boil. Whisk in grits. Cover and reduce heat. Simmer on low for 5 minutes stirring occasionally. Add Cheddar, and butter. Stir until cheese and butter melt. Pour mixture into a lightly greased 13 x 9-inch oven proof baking dish. Sprinkle with parmesan cheese. Bake in a preheated 350° oven for 25-30 minutes.
Serves 6.

Beefy Nacho Cheese Bake

Mother's recipe file contained this recipe. It's easy and good.

1 pound ground sirloin
½ cup chopped onion
¼ teaspoon salt
1/8 teaspoon black pepper
1 tablespoon chili powder
1 teaspoon ground cumin
1 teaspoon dried oregano
1 can condensed Nacho Cheese Soup, undiluted
1 cup milk
1 can Crescent Roll dough
¼ cup shredded cheddar cheese
Chopped fresh cilantro, optional
Salsa, optional

Preheat oven to 375°. Spray a 13 X 9-inch baking dish. Place the onion, and ground sirloin in a large skillet. Sprinkle with the salt and pepper and cook until beef is no longer pink. Drain if there is any fat. Stir in the chili powder, cumin, and oregano. Cook and stir another 2 minutes. Remove from the heat. Combine the soup and milk in a medium bowl, stirring until smooth. Pour the soup mixture into the baking dish and spread evenly.

Separate the crescent roll dough into 4 rectangles. Press perforations together. Roll out each rectangle to 8 x 4-inches. Cut each rectangle in half crosswise to form 8 (4-inch) squares. Spoon about ¼ cup of the beef mixture in the center of each square. Lift 4 corners of dough up over filling to meet in the center. Pinch and twist firmly to seal. Place squares in the baking dish on top of cheese.

Bake uncovered for 20-25 minutes or until crusts are golden brown. Sprinkle cheese over squares. Bake for 5 minutes or until cheese melts. To serve, spoon soup mixture over the beef squares and sprinkle with cilantro, and salsa. Serves 4.

Mexican Lasagna

This is a personal chef dish that even my high profile clients liked. Even though most of them had eaten in the best restaurants all over the world, they still liked good home-made food.

2 pounds ground sirloin
2 teaspoons minced garlic
1 medium onion, finely chopped
1 (3.5 ounce) can sliced black olives
1 (4-ounce) can diced green chilies
1 (10-ounce) can diced tomatoes with green chilies (milder if you like mild)
1 (16-ounce) jar taco sauce
2 (16-ounce) cans refried beans or black beans (drained and mashed) if you prefer the flavor
12 (8-inch) flour tortillas
9 ounce Jack cheese or sharp Cheddar

In a large skillet, sauté the ground beef until almost done. Add the onions and garlic, and sauté until the meat is no longer pink and the onions are transparent. Mix in the olives, green chilies, taco sauce and refried beans. Mix thoroughly and cook on low heat until heated through.
Spray a large baking dish with cooking spray. Spread a layer of meat mixture on the bottom. Add a layer of tortillas, layer of meat and layer of cheese. Keep layering until all of the meat is used. Top with more cheese. Bake in a preheated 350° oven for 25-30 minutes or until bubbly. Serve with sour cream, and guacamole and more cheese. Makes 12 servings.

Mother's Best Meatloaf

This is the meatloaf recipe that mother used. It is so good! The topping makes the meatloaf a little sweet.

2 eggs
2/3 cup milk
3 slices bread, torn into pieces
½ cup chopped onion
½ cup grated carrot
1 cup shredded cheddar or mozzarella cheese
1 tablespoons chopped fresh parsley or 1 teaspoon dried
1 teaspoon salt
1 teaspoon of dried basil, or thyme (optional)
¼ teaspoon pepper
1-½ pounds lean ground beef

Topping

½ cup tomato catsup
½ cup packed brown sugar
1 teaspoon prepared mustard

In a large bowl, beat eggs. Add milk, bread and let stand until the milk has been absorbed into the bread. Stir in the onion, carrot, cheese and seasonings. Add beef and mix well. In a shallow baking dish shape the meat mixture into a loaf. Bake at 350° for 45 minutes. Spoon some of the topping over the meatloaf and bake another 30 minutes longer until it is not pink, occasionally basting with the remaining topping. Let stand 10 minutes before serving. Serving size varies. **Make two and freeze one for another night. Or slice the remaining meatloaf and freeze for another night.

Salisbury Steak

1 egg
1 can (10-1/2 ounce) condensed French Onion Soup, undiluted, divided
½ cup dry bread crumbs
½ teaspoon salt
Pepper to taste
1-1/2 pounds ground sirloin
1 tablespoon flour
¼ cup water
½ cup catsup
1 teaspoon Worcestershire sauce
½ teaspoon prepared mustard

In a large bowl, beat egg. Stir in 1/3 cup of the soup, bread crumbs, salt and pepper. Add beef; mix gently. Shape into 6 small or 3 large oval patties. Brown the meat patties in a skillet over medium heat for 3-4 minutes on each side. Remove and set aside. In the skillet, combine the flour and water until smooth. Add the catsup, Worcestershire sauce, mustard and remaining soup; bring to a boil. Cook and stir for 2 minutes. Return patties to skillet. Cover and simmer for 15 minutes or until meat is no longer pink. Serve on rice or noodles. Serves 6.
Note: Serve with white rice or Mother's yellow rice.

Steve's Favorite Shepard's Pie

We had this at my mother's when we visited. I thought my husband was going to eat the whole thing! He asked my mother for the recipe so I could make it for him at home. Of course she was thrilled that her son-in-law wanted her recipe!

2-1/2 pounds potatoes, peeled and cooked
1 to 1-1/2 cups sour cream
Salt and pepper to taste
2 pounds ground sirloin
½ cup chopped onion
1 small red bell pepper chopped
1 teaspoon garlic salt
1 can (10-3/4 ounce) condensed cream of mushroom soup, undiluted
1 (16-ounce) can whole kernel corn, drained
½ cup milk
2 tablespoon butter

Mash potatoes with sour cream. Add salt and pepper to taste. Set aside. In a skillet, brown the beef with the onion, and red bell pepper until the meat is browned.
Drain if needed. To the meat, add in the garlic salt, soup, corn, and milk. Mix well. Spread meat mixture in a 13 x 9-inch baking dish. Top with mashed potatoes; drizzle with butter. Bake uncovered at 350° for 30-35 minutes or until heated through and bubbly.

Baked Swiss Steak

2 pounds top round (1-inch thick)
1/3 cup all-purpose flour
¼ teaspoon salt
¼ teaspoon pepper
3 tablespoons olive oil
4 stalks celery, sliced into ½ inch pieces
3 carrots, scraped and sliced into 1/2-inch pieces
1 large onion, coarsely chopped
1 green pepper, sliced into thin strips
1 (28-ounce) can diced tomatoes
1 (8-ounce) can tomato sauce
1/3 cup catsup
1 tablespoon Worcestershire sauce
2 teaspoons prepared horseradish (optional)
¼ teaspoon salt
1/8 teaspoon pepper

Add the ¼ teaspoons salt and pepper to the flour. Dredge the steak in the flour. Add the olive oil to a large skillet over medium high heat. Brown the steak in the olive oil. Remove the steak to an oven proof baking dish. Top with the vegetables. In a medium bowl, combine the tomatoes, tomato sauce, Worcestershire sauce, catsup, salt and pepper (horseradish if desired). Pour this mixture over the steak and vegetables. Cover tightly and bake in a pre-heated 325° oven for 2 hours or until the meat is very tender. Serves 4-6.

Chicago Stuffed Cabbage

I don't know where I got this recipe. It was hand-written and stuck inside my notebook that is years old. But, I can tell you that it makes the best stuffed cabbage that I've ever eaten. It's a little work, but if you make it your family will know that you went to some trouble for them.

Stuffing:
½ cup long grain white rice
2 pounds lean ground chuck
1 large onion, finely chopped
3 cloves garlic, finely chopped
1 tablespoon salt
¼ teaspoon freshly ground pepper

Cooking Sauce:
2 cups catsup
½ cup brown sugar, packed
4 cloves garlic, crushed
1 teaspoon salt
2 cups water

Cabbage leaves:
2 large green heads cabbage
3 large onions, chopped

Parboil rice for 7-10 minutes. Drain the rice and mix with the ground beef, onion, garlic, salt and pepper. Set aside.
Mix together the catsup, brown sugar, garlic, salt and water. Set aside.
Bring a very large pot of water to a boil. Use a sharp knife to cut the cores put of the cabbages. Boil each cabbage for 10 minutes. Remove and cool under cool running water. Drain carefully. Peel away the large outer leaves until you get to the inner cabbage leaves that look too small to stuff. You want to have about 26 large cabbage leaves for stuffing. Chop the small inner cabbage leaves into chunks.
Place half the cut up cabbage together with half the chopped onions on the bottom of a large, heavy duty Dutch oven or roasting pan.
Preheat the oven to 375°.
Stuff the cabbage leaves by placing a spoonful of meat mixture in the center of each leaf. Fold over the ribbed end of the leaf, then fold over the two sides and roll up. Place each cabbage roll, fold side down on top of the onion, cabbage mixture in the Dutch oven. When all the cabbage leaves have been

stuffed and packed into the pot (there will be one or two layers, depending on pot size), place the rest of the chopped cabbage and onions over the cabbage rolls. Pour sauce over all, cover tightly and bake for 1-1/2 to 2 hours, until the cabbage is very tender and the sauce has darkened. Place the cabbage rolls in a deep serving platter and cover with the sauce. Serve with boiled potatoes and country bread. Serves 6-8.

Spaghetti MY Way!

1 pound ground sirloin
1 large onion, chopped
2 stalks celery, chopped
1/4 cup chopped green bell pepper
1 teaspoon chopped garlic or ¼ teaspoon garlic powder
2 (14.5 oz.) cans Italian stewed tomatoes or diced Italian tomatoes
2 cans water (use tomato cans)
2 tablespoons chili powder
1 teaspoons dried basil
1 tablespoon salt or to taste
*12 ounces spaghetti
2 cups shredded sharp Cheddar cheese

In a heavy pan or large Dutch oven, sauté ground sirloin until no longer pink. Add onions, pepper, celery, and garlic and continue to cook until vegetables are tender. Add the tomatoes. Add the cans of water, and seasonings. Bring to a boil. *Add the spaghetti making sure that you don't add more than 12 ounces or the sauce will be too dry. Cover and cook on low heat, stirring occasionally, until the spaghetti is cooked. Check to see if it needs more salt, and if it does add it. Cover the top of the spaghetti with the cheese and let the cheese melt before serving. Note: This dish can be frozen.

Janice Rogers Really Good Spaghetti

We were visiting my home in Alabama, and my step-mother made this dish knowing that my husband's favorite food is spaghetti. It was absolutely the best. We just couldn't get enough! I've made it many times since, alternating my easy spaghetti with this one because they are both easy, and both good.

1 pound ground sirloin
1 (16 ounce) package spaghetti
1 large jar Spicy Red Pepper spaghetti sauce
½ jar water
1 package dry spaghetti sauce mix
1 (14.5 ounce) can petite diced tomatoes
Freshly grated parmesan cheese

In a Dutch oven, brown the beef. Add the jar of spaghetti sauce, water, seasoning package of spaghetti sauce mix, and tomatoes. Simmer for 1 hour.
Cook spaghetti according to package directions. Serve the sauce over spaghetti with freshly grated parmesan.

Sara's Vacation Corned Beef & Spaghetti

I think that the name of this dish needs no explanation.
But, I'll give you one! My sister Margaret and I occasionally got this dish when Sara was away on vacation! This one is really good! My son's Rob and Ed like this one as much as I do!

1 can corned beef
2 (16-ounce cans) spaghetti with tomato sauce and cheese
(I think that Campbell's makes it now)

Preheat the oven to 350°. Place the spaghetti in an oven-proof casserole dish. Put the corned beef in the center and pull the corned beef slightly apart.
Bake for 30-40 minutes or until the spaghetti is bubbly and heated through.

Sausage Creole

Easy and good!

1 package smoked sausage, sliced into ½- inch slices
2 tablespoons olive oil
1/3 cup chopped onion
1/3 cup chopped celery
1/3 cup chopped green bell pepper
1 package Spanish Rice Mix
1 (10-ounce) can tomatoes and peppers
¾ cup water
½ teaspoon salt or to taste
¼ teaspoon pepper
1/8 teaspoon cayenne pepper

In a Dutch oven or heavy pan, sauté the onion, bell pepper, and celery in olive oil. Add the rice mix, sliced sausage, and remaining ingredients. Bring to a boil, stirring well. Reduce heat, cover and simmer until the liquid is absorbed, and rice is tender. Remove from the stove and keep covered for about 5 minutes longer. Serves 4.

Chicken

Tombigbee River Fried Chicken

I think that one of the most versatile foods on the earth just happens to be a southern favorite. I'm talking about fried chicken. It is certainly my favorite food.

One cannot think about food in his or her lifetime without thinking of fried chicken and how it has been involved with our emotions. Sunday dinners would never have been the same without a platter of golden brown chicken gracing the table when church was over. Or, the plate of fried chicken that was delivered to your home in a time of sympathetic need. Then there is dinner on the ground, and family reunions and picnics.

It used to be that one of my favorite times for fried chicken was our picnics on the river. Daddy would get the boat out when the weather started to get warm and we'd spend every Sunday afternoon on the river skiing. Mother always had a big cooler with fried chicken, potato salad, pimiento and cheese, fresh pineapple and assorted desserts. The picnic basket was full of dishes and a table clothe. About mid afternoon, daddy would find a sand bar and pull the boat up, and Mother would get out the tablecloth and food and we would "go to town" on that delicious feast. There was nothing like sitting out on that river bank having a picnic.

Those days on the river are long gone, daddy put the boat away years ago, and now my favorite picnic time is with my children and grandchildren. Sometimes now, we picnic at a park on the Ashley River, or on the beach or up at Caesar's Head. But, wherever we are, I am grateful for my time with them.

In all the food trends, fried chicken has never gone out of style. It is much easier to make now than in my grandmother's time. You would have to kill your own chicken, or drive miles from the country to the grocery store. There weren't many restaurants around either, and there were none in my hometown.

So, get out the cooler and the picnic basket and pack it up with the best food from the south. I've given you a slaw recipe (see index for Mother's Sweet Onion Slaw) that mother made in the past few years, or use your mom's favorite recipe. Make sure you don't forget that good old pimiento and cheese and some fresh fruit to go with your basket of chicken!

Enjoy!

Fried chicken is certainly easy enough to make. Wash your chicken really well. (If you have the time, salt it and place it in a bowl of ice water and put it in the refrigerator for several hours.

When ready to fry, drain and rinse. Salt and pepper again. And, while the chicken is still slightly wet, dip it in a mixture of 2 cups self-rising flour, 1 tsp. salt and pepper and ½ tsp. each paprika and thyme. (Make sure that flour covers the entire surface because water will make hot fat splatter everywhere).

Fry the coated chicken in hot oil and if you have a thermometer even better. Your oil should not be below 350°. Add the chicken slowly so that it does not cool the oil. Cook until the juices are clear.

Asian Sesame Chicken

This baked chicken is made with a salad dressing marinade. It's so delicious you won't believe it!

4 boneless, skinless, chicken breast halves
1 (12-ounce) bottle Roasted Asian Sesame Dressing (I used Cardini's)

Place chicken breast in a plastic bag with 3/4 cup dressing. Refrigerate for several hours or overnight. Place chicken and marinade in a foil lined baking dish and bake in a 350° oven for 45 minutes or until juices in chicken run clear. If you would like to grill the chicken, discard marinade, grill until juices run clear. Serves 4.

Cuban Chicken

Serve this with black beans, rice and fresh pineapple.

4 boneless, skinless chicken breast
1 (16-ounce) jar Newman's Own Salsa with Black Beans

Place the chicken breast in an oven-proof dish.
Pour the salsa over the top.
Cover tightly and place in a 350° preheated oven and cook for 45 minutes to an hour. Take the cover off the last 10 minutes of cooking.

Chicken Dijon

This is good for a dinner party.

6 boneless, skinless, chicken breast halves
5 tablespoons butter
3 tablespoons flour
1-1/2 cups chicken stock or broth
¾ cup heavy cream
3 tablespoons Dijon mustard or for texture, Country Dijon mustard

Brown the chicken breast halves in butter for about 15-20 minutes or until the juices are clear. Remove them to a warm platter. Stir the flour into the skillet that the chicken has been cooked in. Cook the flour for about 2 minutes. Add the chicken broth and the heavy cream, and cook until thickened. Add the mustard. Pour the sauce over the warm chicken. Serves 6.

Chicken La Venezia

4 boneless, skinless chicken breasts halves
4 slices Provolone cheese
Fresh spinach leaves
4 slices country ham
Freshly grated Parmesan cheese

Preheat oven to 350°. Place heavy plastic wrap over the chicken breast and pound the breast until thin. Place a slice of Provolone, about 5 spinach leaves, and the country ham on the chicken breast. Sprinkle with Parmesan cheese. Roll-up and secure with a toothpick. Place the chicken in an oven-proof baking dish. Cover with your favorite marinara sauce or Alfredo sauce and cook for 45-60 minutes until chicken is thoroughly cooked. Remove the toothpick before serving. Serves 4.

Goat Cheese and Basil Stuffed Chicken Breasts with Red Pepper Cream Sauce

One of my cooking class favorites!

2/3 cup goat cheese
6 tablespoon fresh chopped basil
2 tablespoons freshly squeezed lemon juice
1/8 teaspoons Salt and pepper
6 small chicken breasts halves (or boneless with skin)
4 tablespoons melted butter
1 minced garlic clove
4 tablespoons olive oil

Red Pepper Cream Sauce:
3 small red peppers, cut in half and seeded
3/4 cup white wine such as Chablis
3 tablespoons white vinegar
1/4 teaspoon chicken granules
2 teaspoons sugar
1-3/4 cups heavy cream
Salt

To make the goat cheese stuffing: Combine the goat cheese, lemon juice, basil, salt and pepper.
Divide the goat cheese mixture between the 6 chicken breast.
This will be just a little over a tablespoon for each breast. Pull back the skin on top of the breast. Place the goat cheese mixture under the skin and pull the skin over it.
In a large skillet, over medium heat, melt the butter; add the olive oil and garlic. Sauté the chicken breast side until the chicken is lightly brown. Place the chicken breast on a baking sheet, skin side up and bake in a preheated 375° oven for 35-40 minutes or until he internal temperature of the breast is 180°, and juices in the chicken breast run clear.
For the red pepper cream sauce: Preheat the broiler. Line a baking pan with foil. Lay the red pepper halves with the skin side up. Place under the broiler and broil until the skin turns black. Remove from the oven and cover with foil. This will steam the peppers and make the skin easy to remove. When you can handle the peppers, remove the skin by rubbing with your fingers or a towel.
Place the peppers, white wine, and vinegar in a saucepan and cook to reduce by half. Add the chicken granules, sugar and cream. Cook until the sauce thickens, about 8 minutes. Transfer the sauce to a blender and puree or use a hand held emulsifier and puree the sauce until smooth.
To serve: Place a large spoon of the sauce on a plate. Place the chicken breast on top and serve.
Note: This sauce can also be used as a sauce for fried green tomatoes.

Southern White House Chicken

The recipe for Southern White House Chicken is one of my cooking class favorites. Serve this with the Orange & Pear Salad.

½ cup all-purpose flour
1 teaspoon salt
1 teaspoon pepper
4 boneless, skinless chicken breast halves cut in half crosswise
Vegetable oil for frying
1 large onion, chopped
1 large green pepper, sliced thin
1 clove garlic, minced
2 (16-ounce) can diced tomatoes, undrained
½ cup currants (or raisins if currants are not available)
¾ teaspoon salt
½ teaspoon pepper
1 tablespoon fresh thyme
2-1/2 teaspoons curry powder
1-1/2 tablespoons chopped fresh parsley
½ cup sliced almonds, toasted

Combine the first three ingredients. Flour the chicken. Add oil to a large skillet and let the temperature reach 350°. Fry the chicken in the hot oil until brown. Drain on paper towels.
Place the chicken in an ovenproof baking dish.
Drain the pan drippings saving about 2 tablespoons of oil in the pan. Cook the onions, peppers and garlic in the drippings until vegetables are tender. Add the tomatoes and the next five ingredients; stir well. Spoon the sauce over chicken in the baking dish. Cover and bake at 350° for 40-50 minutes or until chicken is tender. Transfer chicken to a serving platter. Spoon the sauce over the chicken. Sprinkle with parsley and toasted almonds. Serve the chicken over white rice with salad or fruit. Serves 4.

Chicken with Lemon Sauce

1 tablespoon dry sherry
1 tablespoon soy sauce
½ teaspoon salt
6 skinless, boneless chicken breast halves
2 large eggs, beaten
¼ cup cornstarch
½ teaspoon baking powder
2 cups vegetable oil

Sauce:
1 cup chicken broth
1/3 cup sugar
1 tablespoon cornstarch
1 tablespoon lemon juice
1 teaspoon salt
2 tablespoons vegetable oil
1 lemon, thinly sliced

Chicken: combine the sherry, soy sauce and salt in a large plastic bag. Add the chicken and place the bag in the refrigerator to marinate for 30 minutes.

Combine the eggs, ¼ cup cornstarch and baking powder in a large bowl; stir well. Dip the chicken into the batter, coating well.

Pour 2 cups of the oil into a heavy skillet. Fry the chicken in hot oil over medium-high heat until golden brown. Drain. Cut the chicken breast into quarters and arrange on a platter. Pour the sauce over the chicken.

Sauce: Combine the chicken broth and the next 4 ingredients. Place 2 tablespoons oil in a large skillet over medium high heat. Add the lemon slices and stir-fry them for 30 seconds. Add the broth mixture and cook until sauce is thickened. Pour over the chicken and serve. Serves 6.

Sour Cream Chicken Enchiladas

1 dozen large flour tortillas
1 (4-ounce) can chopped green chilies
8 ounces sour cream
2 cans cream of chicken soup
1 (5-ounce) can evaporated milk
1 milk can water
1 bunch chopped green onions
3 cups chopped cooked chicken
10 ounces grated sharp cheddar cheese

Heat the soup, milk, water, sour cream, onions, and chilies together until bubbling. Add the chicken. Warm the tortillas in the microwave. Ladle about 2 tablespoons of the chicken mixture into the tortilla, top with a spoon of cheese and fold. Place in a 13 x 9-inch casserole dish. Keep rolling the tortillas with the chicken mixture until all the tortillas have been used. Pour the remaining chicken mixture on the tortillas. Top with cheese and bake in a preheated 350° oven until cheese has melted and enchiladas are bubbly.

Note: This is a personal chef recipe and can be frozen for up to 3 months. Thaw in the refrigerator overnight, and cook the following day.

Personal Chef Chicken & Wild Rice Casserole

Okay, now you've got it. One of my most popular personal chef dishes!

1 medium onion, chopped
1 cup finely chopped celery
2 tablespoons butter
5 large boneless, skinless chicken breast halves, cooked and chopped
1 (6-ounce) package long grain and wild rice, cooked
1 teaspoon curry powder
1 (4 ounce) jar pimientos
2 cups mayonnaise
1 can cream of celery soup
1 teaspoon salt or to taste
1 cup water chestnuts
2 (14.5 ounce) cans French style green beans, drained
1 cup grated Cheddar cheese
1 small can pitted and sliced black olives
Paprika

Sauté onion and celery in the 2 tablespoons butter in large skillet or Dutch oven. Add all ingredients except paprika, olives and cheese. Mix thoroughly and pour into greased 4 quart baking dish. Sprinkle with grated cheese, sliced olives and paprika.
Bake in a preheated 350° degree oven for about 45 minutes or until bubbly in the center. You can easily divide this casserole into two casseroles and freeze the second one.

Well Worth It Chicken Pie

My grandmother Irene made the most delicious chicken pie. This one is a little like hers but I put biscuits on top, and she put a crust on top.

1 (3 to 3.5 lb.) chicken
Salt and pepper
Water
3 tablespoons butter
3 tablespoons Flour
¼ teaspoon thyme
1 cup half and half
4 cups chicken broth
1 cup frozen or fresh petite green peas
1-9 inch pie crust
Mary B's Brand Tea Biscuits in the bag

Find a deep pot that the chicken fits in with a little room on the sides. Cover with water ¾ of the way up the sides of the chicken. Add 1 teaspoon salt and a couple of sprinkles of pepper. Cook the chicken, covered, on a simmer for about an hour and a half until the chicken starts to fall off the bone. Turn the heat off and let the chicken sit in the water for another 30 minutes. Then remove the chicken and pull the chicken off the bone, discarding the bones and any skin. Set the chicken aside.
Place butter in a large pot. Let it sizzle and then add the flour. Whisk for about 2 minutes until the flour is cooked. Add the chicken broth slowly, and whisk while adding the broth. Add the half and half, thyme, peas and chicken. Adjust for salt and pepper at this time. Let the mixture cook over medium heat, stirring so it doesn't burn, until it is thickened.
Place the pie crust in the bottom and up the sides of a 2 quart casserole dish. It won't fit all the way up and that is okay. Pour the thickened chicken mixture into the dish. Top with enough tea biscuits to cover the top. Bake in a preheated 350° degree oven until the biscuits are browned. This will take about 35-45 minutes. You can also place the chicken mixture in a 9 X 13 baking dish without the pie crust, and just put biscuits on top.

Mother's Creamed Chicken & Southern Spoon Bread

½ cup chopped celery
¼ cup butter
1/3 cup flour
1 (10-3/4 ounce) can condensed chicken broth
2 cups cubed, cooked chicken
2 tablespoons chopped pimiento
Salt
Parsley

Cook celery in butter until tender but not browned. Blend in the flour. Stir in the condensed chicken broth. Cook and stir until thickened and bubbly. Add the chicken, pimiento and salt to taste. Heat through. Serve over hot spoon bread. Garnish with parsley. Serves 6.

Southern Spoon bread

1 cup white cornmeal
1-1/2 cups boiling water
1 cup milk
2 teaspoons baking powder
1 teaspoon salt
2 eggs lightly beaten
2 tablespoons butter

Slowly pour the boiling water over the cornmeal, stirring until smooth. Stir in the butter and salt. Let cool slightly. Add milk and beaten eggs. Mix well and lastly fold in baking powder. Pour into a lightly-greased baking dish and bake at 375-400° for 40 minutes or until browned.
Note: I use a soufflé dish. It's the perfect size and shape.

Chicken & Ham Casserole

8 ounces spaghetti, broken into 1-inch pieces, cooked
3 cups diced chicken
1 cup diced ham
½ cup chopped pimiento
½ cup chopped green pepper
2 (10 3/4-ounce) can cream of chicken soup
1 cup chicken broth
¼ teaspoon celery salt
¼ teaspoon freshly ground black pepper
1 large finely chopped or grated onion (food processor is good for this)
2 cups grated Cheddar cheese—divided

Mix all ingredients together except 1 cup of cheese. Pour into a sprayed 3 quart casserole or 2 (1.5-quart) casseroles. Sprinkle with remaining cheese.
Bake at 350° for 1 hour. A 3-quart casserole serves 15.
Note: Separate into two 1-1/2 quart casseroles and freeze one casserole and cook one. To thaw, leave in the fridge overnight the night before you are planning to cook it.

Easy Chicken Divan

This recipe has been around for awhile. Lots of people that I know have been making it for years. It's delicious. If you haven't had this, you will wonder why you waited so long to make it.

3 boneless, skinless chicken breasts or 6 boneless, skinless chicken breasts halves
2 (10-ounce) packages frozen broccoli
2 (10-3/4 ounce) cans cream of chicken soup
1 cup sour cream
1 cup mayonnaise
1 cup shredded cheddar cheese
1 tablespoon lemon juice
1 teaspoon curry powder
Salt and pepper to taste
Parmesan cheese
Paprika

Cook chicken breast. Cook broccoli in salted water. Mix soup, sour cream, mayonnaise, lemon juice, grated cheddar, curry and salt and pepper.
Drain broccoli and arrange on the bottom of a buttered 3 quart casserole or two 1-1/2 quart casseroles. Sprinkle generously with Parmesan cheese. Cut chicken into bite size pieces or pull chicken apart and spread over the broccoli. Sprinkle again with Parmesan cheese. Pour sauce over all. Sprinkle with Parmesan cheese and Paprika. Bake at 350° for 30-40 minutes or until bubbly and hot through.
Note: This casserole can be made and frozen. Thaw in the refrigerator overnight and cook the next day.

Italian Chicken

I made this plain, simple and delicious recipe one Sunday night when Joyce McCarrell brought over her pasta machine. It was delicious with home-made pasta.

4 boneless, skinless chicken breasts halves
2 (14.5-ounce) cans Petite diced tomatoes
1/2 cup Balsamic & Basil Vinaigrette (I used Ken's)
½ teaspoon dried basil or 2 tablespoons chopped fresh basil

Place the chicken breast in a glass baking dish. Add the diced tomatoes and Balsamic & Basil Vinaigrette. Bake in a preheated 350°oven for 45-60 minutes or until juices in chicken run clear. Add additional basil before serving. Serves 4.

Sarah's Smothered Chicken

Sometimes, when Sarah fried chicken, she would set the fried chicken aside, and make gravy with the fat and some flour. She poured out all but 3-4 tablespoons of the drippings from cooking the chicken, and added 3 tablespoons flour. She let the flour sizzle in the hot fat, scraping up any bits on the bottom of the skillet. She would cook the flour for a couple of minutes and then add water or chicken broth. About 2 cups I think. The she would add a large onion sliced and then add the chicken back and cover it. It simmered for another 20-30 minutes until the chicken absorbed the gravy and became soft and tender. Before serving she always added enough salt and pepper to season it well.

She served the smothered chicken and gravy over rice and it was delicious!

Pork

Traditions of Easter

(Written in 2000)
I remember my childhood Easter Sunday's very well. My sister Margaret and I usually went to church on Easter morning and after dinner went on an Easter egg hunt. Of course our midday meal was called "dinner" back in those days, and is a seldom used word for the midday meal now. I hate to say that we just couldn't wait to get out of church to eat the wonderful food that waited for us. So, as soon as church was over, we ran home as fast as we could. We must have been a sight from my mother and daddy's perspective as they watched us coming down the lane with one gloved hand holding a purse and another trying to keep our Easter bonnets from flying off.

We were lucky enough to have Sarah in our lives to cook for us back then, but mother always got involved with the holiday cooking and the two of them made this incredibly delicious Sunday dinner. Mother made these delicious English peas and potatoes with white sauce, and some new food ideas too! Mother cooked more and more over the years, and today she is an excellent cook. Still cooking up the same traditional holiday food our family had way back then. Like any good daughter with her own family, I have developed some food traditions of my own.

Baked Ham with Brown Sugar-mustard

My Favorite Ham—I use a boneless ham these days. Make sure that your ham is on a foil lined baking dish. Make scores in the ham's surface. Mix equal amounts of brown sugar and yellow mustard to make a paste. Using your hands, smear the mustard mixture all over the ham. Bake at 350 until cooked through. Baste during baking. The ham will get very dark, but the flavor will be delicious. Use your imagination! Add some pineapple, or apple cider to the paste.

Pork Chops with Baby Bella Mushroom Stuffing & Tomato Vinaigrette

4-double thick pork chops—with a pocket sliced into the side

Marinade:
¾ cup Worcestershire sauce
¾ cup balsamic vinegar
4-1/2 tablespoons minced garlic

Stuffing:
¼ cup olive oil
6 tablespoons finely chopped rosemary
6 cups chopped baby portabellas
4 cups water
2 cups fine fresh bread crumbs

Vinaigrette:
1-1/2 cups olive oil
5 tablespoons finely chopped rosemary
15 sun-dried tomatoes in olive oil
3/4 cup balsamic vinegar

Mix marinade. Place pork chops in a glass dish or plastic zipper bag and marinate for 3 hours or overnight.

Make the stuffing by heating the oil in a large skillet. Add the rosemary and mushrooms and cook until tender. Add the water, and simmer for 5 minutes. Stir in the breadcrumbs and season to taste with salt and pepper. Set aside.

When ready to cook, remove the meat from the marinade. Fill the chops with stuffing. Place the chops in a greased baking dish and bake in a preheated 375° oven for 20 minutes or until juices run clear in chops. (Make sure that pork chops are at least 155 degrees internally).

For vinaigrette, warm the olive oil in a skillet. Add the rosemary, tomatoes, and balsamic vinegar. Remove from heat and puree until smooth. Set aside to keep warm until chops are removed from the oven. To serve, place chops on a platter and pour the warm vinaigrette over them.

Dick's Pork Chops with Vegetables

This is a good simple dish.

6 Center cut pork chops
1 (16-ounce) bag frozen mixed vegetables
1 can cream of mushroom soup
½ soup can milk
1 tablespoon olive oil
1 tablespoon butter

In a large skillet, melt the butter and add the olive oil. Add the pork chops and brown on both sides. Add the frozen mixed vegetables, the can of cream of mushroom soup and milk. Cover tightly and cook until pork chops are done and vegetables are tender. Serves 4-6.

Barbecued Pork chops

4 lean pork chops (1-inch thick)
4 lemon slices
4 tablespoons catsup
4 tablespoons brown sugar
4 onion slices

Place pork chops in a baking dish. Salt each chop. Top each chop with a lemon slice, then onion slice. Sprinkle each chop with 1 tablespoon brown sugar, then 1 tablespoon catsup. Bake covered in a 350°oven for 1 hour. Uncover and bake 30 minutes. Serves 4.
Note: Prepare these ahead, pop in the oven when you get home with 4 baking potatoes and you have dinner!

Chorizo & Greens

½ pound stemmed and cut collards
10 ounces of stemmed and chopped kale
1-1/2 pounds fresh chorizo
1 teaspoon chopped garlic
5 green onions, sliced thin
Olive oil

Preparation of greens: Remove the stems from the greens. Stack about5 leaves together and fold over. Cut into thin strips, or chop. Wash greens 3 times after chopping them. Place in a colander to drain, but do not dry greens. Leave water on the leaves. This will help them steam.
Slice chorizo into diagonal cuts about 1-inch thick. In a large Dutch oven, sauté chorizo in 1-2 tablespoons olive oil until done.
Add onions and garlic and sauté until caramelized. Remove chorizo and onion mixture to a bowl and set aside. Add greens to the pan that you cooked the chorizo in. Cover and cook on a medium-high heat until greens are tender. When greens are tender add back the chorizo, onion mixture and cook until chorizo is hot. Salt and pepper as needed. Serve immediately.

Chorizo and Peppers

1-1/2 pounds fresh chorizo
1 of each—large red, orange and yellow bell peppers
3 garlic cloves, sliced thin
3-4 fresh thyme or Greek oregano sprigs
Olive oil

Roast chorizo in a preheated 350° oven until the internal temperature of the chorizo reaches 165 degrees. While the chorizo is roasting, cut the peppers into thin strips and set aside.
When the chorizo is done, remove from the oven and set aside to cool enough to slice into 1-inch slices on the diagonal.
Pour 2 tablespoons olive oil into a large skillet. Add the sliced peppers and sauté until the peppers are just getting tender. Add the garlic slices, and the chorizo and herbs. Cook until the peppers are tender. Serve with roasted baby Yukon's. (See index).

Phyllo Pastry Pie with Peppers, Green Onions and Kale

I remember the first time in my life that I had Kale. It was when I went to school at Barton Academy in Mobile. I used to try to figure out what I could swap for it at lunch time! I love the stuff. So, I was delighted to get this recipe from my cooking class at The Greenbrier.

Pie:
¾ cup unsalted butter
1 pound package phyllo dough

For the filling:
1-1/2 pounds Kale
3 medium onions, chopped
½ pound sausage meat
2 tablespoons butter
½ teaspoon ground allspice
Salt and pepper to taste
2 eggs
(If you would like to, you can add 1 cup of ricotta cheese to the kale mixture when it cools).

To make the filling: Wash the kale well and discard any thick stems. Stack the leaves, roll them loosely and cut them into thin strips. Chop the onions. Heat the butter in the frying pan; add the sausage meat and cook, stirring, until crumbled and brown, 3-5 minutes. Transfer to a bowl with a slotted spoon. Add the onions to the frying pan and cook, stirring until soft. Add the kale strips, cover and cook very gently until the kale is wilted, 3-5 minutes. Stir the sausage meat and allspice into the kale mixture and season with salt and pepper to taste. Remove from the heat and let cool completely.
Lightly beat the eggs into a bowl and stir them into the cooled kale mixture.

To assemble the pie:
Heat the oven to 350°. Melt the butter and brush the tart pan with a little bit of the butter. Lay a damp towel on the work surface. Unroll the phyllo dough sheets onto the towel. Using a large plate as a guide, cut rounds of phyllo 3-inches wider that the tart pan that you are using to bake the pie. Reserve the trimmings for decoration. Cover the circles and trimmings with another damp towel. Do not let the phyllo dry out.
Put the phyllo round on top of the moist towel and brush it lightly with butter. Transfer it to a prepared tart pan, pressing it well into the sides. Butter another phyllo round and put it in the pan. Continue buttering and layering until you've used half the rounds. This will equal about 6 or 7 layers of phyllo rounds. Spread the kale mixture evenly over the pastry. Butter another round of phyllo dough,

and cover the kale filling with it. Top with the remaining rounds, brushing each with butter. Brush the top of the last round. Fold the overlapping dough up around the edges of the pie. Cut the dough trimmings into 2-inch strips. Pleat them to form ruffles and arrange them on the pie, so it is completely covered.

Baking the pie: The pie can be baked right away or wrapped in plastic wrap and refrigerated for up to 2 days. It also freezes. Bake the pie in the preheated oven until golden brown for 45-60 minutes. If the pie browns too quickly cover it with foil. Let the pie cool slightly then cut into wedges and serve hot or at room temperature.

Baked Ziti with Mushroom & Sausage

1 pound sweet Italian sausage
1 pound ziti
½ pound mushrooms, sliced
½ cup freshly grated Romano or Parmesan cheese
1 teaspoon salt
1 teaspoon pepper
¼ teaspoon dried oregano
½ teaspoon minced garlic
2 cups tomato sauce (see recipe below)
½ cup freshly grated mozzarella cheese for topping

Preheat the oven to 375° degrees. Place the sausage in a shallow pan, pierce with a fork to help the fat find its way out, and bake until the sausage is browned and cooked through. Cut the sausage into ¼ inch slices. Set aside.

Cook the pasta according to package directions until just al dente. Drain the pasta and place in a mixing bowl. Add the sliced sausage, mushrooms, cheese, salt, pepper, oregano, and garlic. Mix in 1 cup of the tomato sauce. Transfer the mixture to a baking pan and pour the remaining sauce on top. Sprinkle with the bread crumb topping (recipe below.) Bake, uncovered for 45 minutes. Remove from the oven and sprinkle with mozzarella cheese and return to the oven for 10 minutes or until the cheese melts. Serves 4-6

Tomato Sauce:
1/3 cup oil
1 medium onion, finely chopped
2 cloves garlic, minced
1 (28-ounce) can plum tomatoes, chopped or crushed
1 (6-ounce) can tomato paste
6 ounces water-use can to measure
2 tablespoons chopped parsley
1 teaspoon dried basil
1 teaspoon salt
¼ teaspoon pepper
¼ teaspoon dried thyme
Pinch of sugar, if needed

Sauté the onion and garlic in oil. Add remaining ingredients and cook on a simmer for an hour. Freeze any sauce not used for the baked ziti.

Topping:
1 cup bread crumbs
½ cup freshly grated Romano cheese
½ teaspoon salt
¼ teaspoon pepper
¼ teaspoon dried oregano
½ teaspoon minced garlic
2 teaspoon chopped parsley
Combine all ingredients and mix well. Use to top the casserole.

Ham Alfredo with Bow Tie Pasta

1 16-ounce) package bow tie pasta, cooked and drained
1 (10-ounce) package frozen peas
4 tablespoons butter
4 tablespoons flour
3 teaspoons minced garlic
2 cups milk
1 (8-ounce) package cream cheese, softened
½ cup grated parmesan cheese
3 cups cooked ham, cut into thin strips

Heat the butter in saucepan over medium heat. Add garlic and cook for one minute. Whisk in flour and cook for 2 minutes. Add milk, whisking to smooth the sauce. Simmer for three minutes. Whisk in cream cheese and 1/4 cup Parmesan. Simmer, whisking constantly for 3-5 minutes, until smooth and thickened. Remove from heat. Toss together hot pasta, sauce, peas and ham in large bowl. Sprinkle with remaining Parmesan and toss again. Place in an oven-proof baking dish. Bake in a preheated 350°oven until hot and bubbly.

To freeze, place in a container that can be frozen and reheated. Thaw in the refrigerator overnight before cooking. Cook to an internal temperature of 170° degrees or bubbly and thoroughly heated.

Ham & Artichoke Rolls

4 tablespoons butter
4 tablespoons flour
2 cups warm milk
Dash salt and pepper
¼ teaspoon nutmeg
Pinch paprika
2/3 cup shredded Swiss cheese
2/3 cup freshly grated Parmesan
4 tablespoons sherry
2 (8.5 ounce) cans artichoke hearts, drained
12 thick slices baked or boiled ham

Topping:
2/3 cup bread crumbs
2/3 cup freshly grated Parmesan
1/3 cup shredded Swiss cheese

Preheat oven to 350°. Butter a 9 x 9-inch baking dish.
Melt the butter in a medium saucepan over medium high heat. Stir in flour and whisk until smooth. Remove from the heat and add the warmed milk. Return to heat, stirring constantly until thickened. Add salt and pepper, nutmeg and paprika. Add cheeses and stir until melted. Remove from heat and stir in sherry. Cut artichoke hearts in half. Wrap two halves, end to end in a slice of ham. Arrange, seam side down with sides touching in the dish. Pour sauce over the ham. Combine bread crumbs and cheeses and sprinkle over the top. Bake for 30-35 minutes.

Greek Pork Tenderloin with Sun-dried Tomatoes, Spinach and Fresh Herbs

I wish I could say where this recipe came from so that I could give them credit, but I don't have a clue.

Judy Booker asked me to teach a Greek class back in 2004, and I used this recipe for the tenderloin, as well as the Greek Potatoes with Lemon, and the Greek Salad recipe found in the index. I do remember working on the recipe for the tenderloin, but I know that I didn't create the potato recipe. Try them all together for a nice Greek dinner.

1 package pork tenderloins (package of 2)
½ (10-ounce) package chopped spinach (thawed and squeezed of excess water)
2 green onions, including tops, thinly sliced
2 teaspoons chopped fresh Greek oregano
1 tablespoon chopped fresh dill
½ cup sun-dried tomatoes in olive oil, drained and finely chopped
1 cup crumbled feta cheese

Cut a slice almost through the center of the pork tenderloins making sure that your knife does not cut all the way through to the other side. Place the tenderloins between sheets of plastic wrap or waxed paper and pound flat.

For the stuffing: Sauté the onion, and spinach in 2 tablespoons olive oil. In another bowl, add the oregano, dill, sun-dried tomatoes and feta cheese. Add the spinach and onions.

Place half the mixture into one tenderloin, and the other half in the other tenderloin. Roll the tenderloins and tie each with string by looping it from end to end. Cook tenderloins in a pre-heated 400° oven until the internal temperature of the tenderloin is 155 degrees. Remove the string, cover and let rest for 10 minutes before slicing. Serve with balsamic sauce.

Balsamic Sauce

1 cup balsamic vinegar
2 tablespoons chopped fresh rosemary
6 cloves chopped fresh garlic
6 tablespoons honey
4 tablespoon olive oil
2 tablespoon Dijon mustard
2 tablespoon butter
Salt and pepper to taste

In a medium saucepan, mix all ingredients except butter, salt and pepper. Cook rapidly until sauce starts to thicken. Remove from heat and add butter, one tablespoon at a time. Add salt and pepper to taste.

Marinated Pork Tenderloin

Serve as an entrée with Jezebel Sauce (see index) or sliced thin with party rolls for cocktails.

¼ cup soy sauce
¼ cup Madeira
2 tablespoons olive oil
1 tablespoon dry mustard
1 teaspoon ground ginger
1 teaspoons sesame oil
8 drops hot sauce
2 cloves garlic, minced
½ cup apple cider vinegar
2 (3/4 pound) pork tenderloins

Combine all ingredients except pork tenderloins. Place tenderloins in a plastic bag or a shallow dish with a top. Pour marinade over pork. Refrigerate for 8 hours or over night. Bake in a pre-heated 400°oven until a meat thermometer reaches 160 degrees in the thickest part of the pork. Remove from the oven and let rest for 5-10 minutes before slicing thin. Serves 12-15.

Savory Pork Tenderloin

Package of 2 pork tenderloins
¼ cup oil
1 teaspoon Dijon mustard
2 tablespoons sherry vinegar
2 teaspoons sugar
2 teaspoons salt
1 teaspoons pepper
2 tablespoons fresh thyme

Place the tenderloins in a zippered plastic bag. Mix remaining ingredients in a small bowl. Pour over the tenderloins and refrigerate for several hours or overnight.
Cook in an aluminum lined pan on a wire rack in a 400° oven until the internal temperature has reached 160°. Remove from the oven and wait 5-10 minutes before slicing.

Pork Tenderloin & Apples a la Apple Cider

2 (3/4 pound) pork tenderloins
¾ cup apple cider
½ cup brown sugar
1 tablespoon Creole Mustard
3 apples, peeled, cored and sliced

Place the tenderloins and remaining ingredients except the apples in a plastic bag and marinate for 3 hours or overnight. Remove tenderloins and marinade to a roasting pan lined with foil. Place the apples along the sides of the pork. Roast in a 400° oven until the temperature reaches 160° when a meat thermometer is inserted into the thickest part of the meat. Let rest for 10 minutes before slicing on the diagonal. Remove the apples to a bowl and keep warm until ready to serve.

Seafood

The Road to Inverness

The road to Inverness around Loch Ness was as mysterious as the lake itself. It was shadowed by the hills and mountains on the left with large trees overhanging the road. Down the hill, the lake loomed on the right.

Far, far across the lake, large homes and yacht basins could be seen. The yacht basins were for the tour boats that took out the "Nessie" hunters.

The weather had started to get cloudy and cold, and it appeared that sleet was about to fall on us. This would make the road even more dangerous and the monster even harder to find. Every time we came to an overlook on the road, we stopped to see if "Nessie" had pulled up to the roadside looking for a handout. Nothing! What could be seen were strange ripples in the water that may appear to be something, if your imagination were to run a little wild.

After finally arriving in Inverness from the long trip around the lake, hunger took away the thoughts of "poor Nessie". Now thinking of food, we spotted a wonderful little restaurant where we ordered fresh salmon. Along with the salmon came mashed potatoes and leeks au gratin. For dessert, we had a slice of lemon tart and cups of tea to prepare us for the weather as we left the warmth of the fireplace and stepped outside into the falling, blowing snow.

Later, tucked into a warm bed, I thought about the perfect meal and the perfect evening that we had enjoyed. Had I died and gone to heaven, yes!

Coquille St. Jacques with Gruyere Mashed Potatoes

This dish may look complicated but it's not! I've been making it for years.

I can't say the name without being reminded by my mother of the correct pronunciation of "Jacque" since I am more likely to say, Jack! This dish is rich, creamy and delicious. It pairs well with the Citrus Salad. I made this for my host and hostess my last night in Ottawa. They loved it. I hope you will too!

1 cup dry white wine
½ teaspoon salt
1 bay leaf
2 tablespoons minced shallot
1 parsley sprig
2 tablespoons minced celery
1-½ pounds bay scallops or if using sea scallops—cut in half*
½ pound fresh mushrooms, sliced
¼ cup fresh lemon juice
3 tablespoons butter
3 tablespoons flour
½ cup milk
2 egg yolks, beaten
¾ cup heavy whipping cream
Dry white wine as needed
Good mashed potatoes (already prepared)
1 cup finely grated Gruyere cheese

*Note: Go around the edge of each scallop and check for the small tough muscle on the round edge. Just pull it off if by chance it has been missed by the fishmonger.

Use 6 scallop shells or a 2 quart casserole or large au gratin dish. In a stainless steel or enameled sauce pan, simmer wine, salt, bay leaf, shallots, parsley and celery for 5 minutes. Remove the bay leaf and parsley.

Wash the scallops. Add scallops to liquid in saucepan. Add water if necessary to cover. Simmer until tender, about 5 minutes. Remove scallops from liquid and boil liquid rapidly to reduce to 1 cup. Preheat oven to broil.

Place mushrooms in a large skillet. Pour the lemon juice over the mushrooms. Cook mushrooms over medium heat until tender.

Melt butter in a medium size saucepan over medium heat. Stir in the flour and cook until smooth and bubbly. Remove from the heat and whisk in the milk, egg yolks, cream and 1 cup liquid from scallops.

Return to the heat to thicken. Thin the sauce with wine if it is too thick. Add scallops and mushrooms to sauce. Check for seasoning and add salt if needed. Divide mixture evenly into the scallop shells or pour into an oven-proof baking dish. Spread mashed potatoes on top of scallop mixture. Sprinkle Gruyere on top of potatoes. Place in a 350° preheated oven and bake until bubbly and cheese is melted.

Note: Because of the lemon juice and wine you should not use a metal pan for this dish.

Salmon

Buy fresh salmon. If it smells like fish, don't buy it. It should smell clean. Some salmon may still have the pin bones. To find out, rub your fingers across the flesh from the tail toward the front or head and if you feel the bones, pull the bones out with tweezers. Most salmon is cleaned, and boned in the store. If you choose not to cut the salmon into serving pieces or to take the skin off if needed, have the fish department at your local grocery store do it for you. Usually servings are 3 ounces for a small appetizer serving and 6-8 ounces for a regular dinner portion.

Asian Sesame Salmon

4 (6-ounce) salmon filets
1 (12-ounce) bottle Roasted Asian Sesame Dressing (I use Cardini's)

Place salmon in a baking dish lined with foil. Pour on ½ cup dressing and bake salmon in a 350°oven, basting frequently. Bake for about 30 minutes or until salmon flakes, or pulls apart easily.

Salmon in Sun-dried Tomato Pesto

4 (6-8-ounce) salmon filets
1 (10-ounce) jar sun-dried tomato pesto (in pasta section of grocery store)
1-1/4 cups milk or cream

Place the salmon in a large sauté pan in melted butter. Let the salmon start to sizzle then turn the heat down, and cover the pan until the salmon is tender and flaky. This will take about 20 minutes. You will know when it is done when you put a fork into the fish and the fish flakes or comes apart easily. (The rule for cooking fish is about 10 minutes per inch of thickness, but I have found that it always takes longer.)
When the fish is done, remove the bottom skin and discard. Add the 1-10oz. jar Classico Sun-Dried Tomato Pesto sauce to the sauté pan with the salmon. Then add 10 ounces of milk. (Just use the jar to measure) (You can use light or low-fat milk, heavy cream, or regular milk). Let the mixture cook, bubbling, until it has blended well and thickened. Remove from heat and serve over polenta (see index) or fettuccine.

Baked Salmon with Seasonings

1 (6-8 ounce) salmon filet per person
Canadian Steak Seasoning
Creole Seasoning (the guy who "kicks it up a notch brand")

Sprinkle each filet with steak seasoning and Creole seasoning mix on both sides. Place filets in a baking dish and place in a 350°preheated oven. Bake for 25-30 minutes or until filets are tender and flaky. Serve immediately.

Salmon Filets with Herb Butter & Mustard Cream Sauce

This is a personal chef recipe that I have been making for several years. It's easy to make and easy to freeze. It's really good, especially with the mustard cream sauce, served with a rice pilaf and citrus salad.

5 tablespoons butter softened
1-1/2 tablespoons chopped fresh tarragon or 1 teaspoon dried
1-1/2 chopped fresh chives
1-1/2 tablespoons chopped fresh parsley
1-1/2 tablespoons chopped shallot
1-1/2 tablespoons Country Dijon Mustard
¼ teaspoon black pepper
6 (6-ounce) salmon filets (skin removed)
See mustard cream recipe below

Combine the first 7 ingredients. Spray a baking dish with cooking spray. Place salmon filets in the baking dish. Spread the butter mixture over each piece of salmon. Bake at 350° for 25-30 minutes until salmon flakes with a fork.

To make the mustard cream sauce: Place salmon on a plate when removed from the oven. Pour the mustard, butter mixture from the salmon into a small skillet. Add 1 cup heavy cream, and more mustard if needed for taste. Cook and reduce the sauce for about 5 minutes. Pour the mustard sauce over the salmon and serve.

Salmon & Eggs over Rice

Another one of "Sarah is on vacation" dishes from my mother. We all loved this one. Mother served the salmon and eggs over rice with hot biscuits and jam or jelly on the side.

1 cup fresh salmon, cooked and flaked
4 eggs
3 tablespoons chopped green onion
3 tablespoons butter
Salt and pepper to taste
4 servings cooked white rice

In a medium bowl, beat the eggs, and salmon.
Melt the butter in a skillet. When the butter is sizzling, add the green onions and cook for 1-2 minutes. Then add the egg mixture and "scramble" just as you would scramble eggs. Add salt and pepper to taste. When eggs are set, serve over white rice with biscuits and a salad. Serves 4.
Note: Back in the piney woods of Alabama we could not get fresh salmon, so we used canned salmon. It tastes just great using the canned salmon.

Salmon Loaf with Cucumber Sauce

This is an easy make ahead dish. Make it, put it in the fridge, and then pop it in the oven before your company arrives. The sauce can be made in advance too!

Loaf:
1 (16-ounce) can salmon flaked and drained
Or 1 pound cooked fresh salmon, flaked
½ cup dry French bread crumbs or commercial bread crumbs
½ cup mayonnaise
½ cup finely chopped red onion
¼ cup finely chopped celery
¼ cup finely chopped green pepper
1-1/2 teaspoons capers, drained
1 egg beaten
3/4 teaspoon salt
1/8 teaspoon pepper

Cucumber Sauce:
½ cup mayonnaise
½ cup sour cream
½ cup chopped cucumber
2 teaspoons chopped green onion
½ teaspoon dried dill weed

Preheat the oven to 350°. Grease a 9 x 5-inch loaf pan.
Loaf: Combine the salmon, breadcrumbs, mayonnaise, onion, celery, green pepper, capers, egg, salt and pepper. Mix until well combined. Place in the loaf pan. Bake for 40 minutes. Serve warm or cool and refrigerate for 2 or more hours to chill down. Slice and serve with sauce.
Sauce: Combine all ingredients and refrigerate until ready to serve Salmon.

Cheesy Shrimp & Grits

My friend Ellen went to a book club meeting and on her way home she called to say that she had just had the BEST shrimp and grits casserole ever for dinner. She had asked for the recipe so that she could make it. She shared the recipe with me.

4 cups chicken broth
½ teaspoon salt
1 cup quick grits (not instant)
1 cup shredded sharp Cheddar cheese, divided
1 cup Mexican cheese mix
2 tablespoons butter
6 green onions, chopped
1 green bell pepper, chopped
1 garlic clove, minced
1 pound small fresh shrimp, peeled
1 (10-ounce) can tomatoes with diced green chilies, drained
¼ teaspoon salt
¼ teaspoon pepper

Bring the chicken broth and ½ teaspoon salt to a boil in a large saucepan. Whisk in the grits. Cover and reduce heat and simmer for 20 minutes. Stir together the grits, and ¾ cup Cheddar and the 1 cup Mexican cheese. Melt butter in a large skillet over medium heat; add the onions, bell pepper, garlic and shrimp and sauté for 5 minutes or until tender. Stir together the grits mixture, shrimp mixture and the next 3 ingredients and pour into a sprayed 2-quart baking dish. Sprinkle the top with the remaining cheese. Bake at 350° for 30-40 minutes or until bubbly.

Creamed Shrimp over Toast Points or Pastry Shells

Roux and sauce:
4 tablespoons butter, melted
2 tablespoons flour
2 cups fat free half and half

Shrimp:
½ cup butter
1 cup diced red bell pepper
2 cups thinly sliced mushrooms
¾ cup white wine
4 cups medium shrimp, peeled and deveined
1 tablespoon fresh chopped tarragon
Freshly grated nutmeg

In a medium saucepan, melt the butter until sizzling. Add the flour and cook for two minutes. Add the half and half and let thicken slightly. In another skillet melt the remaining butter. Add the mushrooms and red pepper and cook until tender. Add the shrimp and cook for about 5 minutes. Add the wine. Add the half and half mixture to the shrimp mixture. Add the tarragon and a dash of freshly grated nutmeg. Serve over toast points or in puff pastry shells. * Add a little more wine if necessary to thin out the sauce.

Gulf Coast Flounder & Artichoke Butter Sauce

I lived in the town of Daphne on Mobile Bay when I was a teenager. I loved living on the water.
I remember a Jubilee happening one night and all these fish came washing up on shore. We ran home and got a frying pan, some bacon and eggs, and built a fire on the beach and cooked breakfast while watching the fish come rolling into shore. We dared not eat the fish that rolled in on the red tide. Serve this with red rice and sweet onion slaw.

6 flounder filets
½ teaspoon salt
½ teaspoon pepper
1 egg, lightly beaten
1 cup milk
¾ cup all-purpose flour
Oil for frying
1 (14-ounce) can artichoke hearts, drained and cut into quarters
1-1/2 cups sliced mushrooms
½ cup butter, melted
1-1/2 teaspoon Worcestershire sauce
1-1/2 teaspoons lemon juice
1-1/2 teaspoons white wine vinegar
½ cup sliced almonds, toasted

Sprinkle filets with salt and pepper on both sides. Combine the egg and milk in a shallow bowl. Dip the filets in the egg, milk mixture, and then in the flour. Heat 2-inches of oil in a deep heavy skillet until oil sizzles then add the fish. Fry filets in the oil and brown on both sides. Drain on paper towels. Keep warm in a warm oven.
Melt the butter in a medium saucepan. Add artichoke hearts and mushrooms. Cook until mushrooms are tender. Add the remaining ingredients and cook for 2 minutes. Serve the sauce over the fish.

Crab Stuffed Pasta Shells with Tomato Cream Sauce

This recipe is "borrowed" from a restaurant in San Francisco.

1-1/2 pounds of crab meat
3 (8-ounce) packages cream cheese
¾ cup freshly grated Parmesan, Asiago, or Romano
1 teaspoon minced garlic
¼ cup finely chopped shallots
Freshly ground pepper to taste
1/3 cup chopped fresh tarragon
½ teaspoon crushed red pepper flakes
8 ounces large pasta shells
2 ripe tomatoes, peeled, seeded and chopped
Grated Parmesan

Cream Sauce:
4 cups heavy cream
2 teaspoons minced garlic
2 tablespoons finely chopped shallots
Salt and pepper to taste

Blend the first 8 ingredients and adjust the seasonings. Cook the pasta shells according to the instructions on the package.

Cream sauce: Prepare the cream sauce by combining all ingredients in a saucepan and heating until the mixture is reduced by half.

Pour the reduced cream sauce into a shallow baking dish that will hold the shells in one layer. Stuff the shells with the crabmeat-cheese mixture; arrange them on top of the sauce, and bake, covered at 400° for 15 to 20 minutes. Remove from the oven and top with the chopped tomato and grated Parmesan cheese.

Cake

A Southern State of Mind

Our great southern states are full of warm and friendly people, and sweet southern towns. It's a place where you are still invited to sit for awhile on the porch, and have a glass of sweet tea, and a piece of cake that has been tucked away by the hostess just waiting for company.

Thank goodness that is the way it was and still is. I hope we never change!

So to put you in a hospitable state of mind, I am giving you a recipe that just gets better with age, if it last that long. And, it's made with the symbol of hospitality, the pineapple.

Pineapple signs have marked garden gates, town welcome signs, teapots, and water towers all across the south. There's even a beautiful little town in Alabama called Pineapple! Welcome, welcome, welcome is the message conveyed. We look forward to your visit! I know your company, and family will look forward to this cake too. My grandmother would say, "well my stars, I didn't know anything could taste so good and be so easy."

Pineapple Cake

I make this cake in layers, but you can also make it in a 13 X 9-inch glass baking dish and it's easier and tastes the same.

Cake:
2 cups sugar
2 cups all-purpose flour
½ cup vegetable oil
2 eggs
1 20-ounce can crushed pineapple with juice (I used Dole)
1 teaspoon baking soda

In a medium bowl combine all of the ingredients. Pour into a well-greased 13 x 9-inch pan. Bake at 350° for 25 + minutes or until a cake tester comes out clean. If you are making a sheet cake, prepare the icing while the cake bakes.

If you are making this cake in layers, use three 9-inch cake pans. Divide the mixture between pans. Bake in a 350°preheated oven for approximately 22 minutes or until a cake tester comes out clean from the center of the cake. When the layers have cooled slightly, spread about ½ cup icing between layers and place the remaining icing on top. If you really want to make it a hit, put 7 minute icing all over the cake.

Icing:
1 cup sugar
½ cup butter, softened
2/3 cup evaporated milk (1 small can)
Pinch of salt
½ cup pecans, chopped
½ cup coconut

In a saucepan combine the sugar, butter, milk and salt. Bring to a boil and then lower the heat. Cook and stir for 10 minutes. Remove the pan from the heat. Add the pecans and coconut. Pour the icing over the hot cake and allow it to cool before cutting. 12-15 servings.

Mommy's Apple Cake

This is my grandmother's apple cake recipe. I was going through some of my mother's papers from 30 years ago and found it hand-written. It's a delicious cake.

3 cups finely diced, peeled apples
1 cup chopped pecans, toasted
2 cups sugar
3 cups self-rising flour
1 cup oil
1 teaspoon vanilla
3 eggs

Beat all together and pour into a Bundt pan. Bake at 350° for 1 hour or until a cake tester comes out clean. Cool in the pan for 10 minutes then turn out on to a wire rack to cool.

Louise's Apple Cake

Louise was my mother's neighbor. Mother always enjoyed this cake.

Cake:
2-1/2 cups self-rising flour
1 cup brown sugar
1 cup sugar
1-1/2 cups oil
3 large eggs
1 teaspoon vanilla
¼ teaspoon cinnamon
4 cups chopped apples
1 cup chopped nuts, toasted
1 cup coconut

Mix all ingredients together and pour into a greased and floured 13 x 9-inch baking dish. Bake at 350° until a cake tester comes out clean. Cover with icing.

Icing:
1 cup brown sugar
¾ stick butter
2 teaspoons milk
1 teaspoon vanilla
Powdered sugar

Boil until the brown sugar has dissolved. Add the vanilla and enough powdered sugar to thicken the icing.

Banana Brown Sugar Pound Cake

Cake:
2 sticks butter
1-1/4 cups light brown sugar, packed
½ cup granulated sugar
5 eggs
1-3/4 cups all-purpose flour
1 teaspoon baking powder
¼ cup milk
1 teaspoon vanilla
1 ripe banana

Foster Sauce:
2 sticks butter
1 pound light brown sugar
3 tablespoons Grand Marnier
1 cup heavy cream
1-2 bananas sliced

Cake: Heat oven to 325°. Grease and flour a 10-inch tube or Bundt pan. Cream butter and sugars until light and fluffy. Add eggs, one at a time, allowing each to be well-mixed. Mix the flour and baking powder together and set aside. Mash banana with milk and vanilla. With the mixer on low speed, add the flour mixture alternating with the banana mixture to the sugar-butter. Continue mixing until the dry ingredients are moistened. Do not over mix. Pour the batter into the pan and place in the center of the oven rack. Bake for 30-40 minutes until golden brown and a tester inserted in the center comes out clean. Cool for 30 minutes.

To make the sauce: Combine the butter and brown sugar. Bring the mixture to a rolling boil. Remove the pan from the heat and immediately add heavy cream and liqueur. Stir to blend well. Allow to cool. Warm sauce and add sliced bananas. Pour sauce over pound cake. Make 16 servings.

The Ultimate Banana Cake with Caramel Icing!

I think this will be the best banana cake with icing that you have put in your mouth! It's from Too Jay's, one of my favorite restaurants in Palm Beach, Florida.

Cake:
1-1/2 sticks butter
1-1/2 cups sugar
2 eggs, beaten
1-1/2 cups all-purpose flour
1 teaspoon baking soda
¼ cup sour cream
2 medium ripe bananas, mashed
1 teaspoon vanilla
1 cup chopped walnuts or pecans, toasted

In a medium bowl cream the butter until fluffy. Gradually add the sugar and mix well. Add the eggs and mix well. In a small bowl, mix together the flour and baking soda with a whisk. Add the flour mixture to the creamed mixture alternately with the sour cream. Blend well. Add the bananas, vanilla and nuts. Mix well. Pour the batter into two 8-inch round cake pans and bake in a preheated 350° oven for 30-35 minutes. Let the cakes cool in pans for 15 minutes, and turn out onto wire racks to finish cooling.
Note: Cakes may sag a little in the middle.

Frosting:
1 stick unsalted butter
1 cup firmly packed light brown sugar
¼ cup milk
1 cup confectioners' sugar, sifted

Melt the butter in a saucepan over medium heat. Add the brown sugar and melt it, stirring constantly for 2 minutes. Remove from the heat. Add the milk and stir to blend. Return to the heat until the mixture begins to bubble at the edges. Cook over medium-low heat, stirring occasionally, for 3 minutes. Do not boil. The mixture should be barely bubbling. Remove from the heat and cool to lukewarm. Add confectioners' sugar. Frost the cake.
Note: Use the nuts to put on top of the cake!

160 Year Old Black Walnut Cake

I made this cake the first time when it was only 125 years old! It's a wonderful recipe to have in the fall when you can easily find black walnuts.

2 sticks butter
½ cup shortening
3 cups sugar
5 eggs
1 teaspoon vanilla
½ teaspoon rum flavoring (optional)
3 cups plain flour
1 cup black walnuts, chopped fine
1 teaspoon baking powder
1 cup cream or half and half

Cream butter and shortening with sugar. Beat well. Add eggs, one at a time, beating well after each egg. Add flavoring and beat again. Mix ½ cup flour with the black walnuts. Set aside. Add remaining flour mixed with baking powder alternately with cream to the creamed mixture, starting and ending with flour. Fold in nuts. Bake in a large greased and floured tube pan for 1 hour and 20 minutes at 325°. Do not open the oven door during the first hour of baking.

Sybil Rogers Caramel Cake

Every year at our family reunion Sybil Rogers brings this caramel cake. This cake is so famous that everyone who knows better will get a piece before they get their lunch, knowing there won't be any left when they finish eating. I can hear my father clearly ask, "Can you get me a piece of Sybil's cake?" And when it arrives, he slips it to the side of his luncheon plate.

My greatest compliments Sybil for a wonderful cake!

Cake:
1 cup Crisco
1-1/4 cups sugar
1 cup milk
4 eggs, beaten
1 teaspoon vanilla
2 cups self-rising flour

Mix sugar and Crisco, mixing well. Add eggs, beating thoroughly. Add vanilla. Add milk and flour alternately, beginning and ending with flour. Mix well. Grease and flour (I use a flour spray such as Baker's Joy) three 9-inch cake pans. Bake 20-22 minutes at 350° or until done.

Frosting:
2 cups sugar
1 small can evaporated milk
½ cup sugar
2 sticks butter or margarine *see note

Mix 2 cups sugar and evaporated milk in a large saucepan on very low heat.
Put the ½ cup sugar in an iron skillet or heavy bottomed pan. Heat the ½ cup sugar until melted and dark brown (burned practically.) Add the caramelized sugar to the sugar and milk mixture, turn up the heat and cook about 10 minutes. Remove from heat and add margarine and stir until ready to spread.
Note: Margarine is better in this recipe than butter because of the water content. I use Imperial.

Larry's Chocolate Birthday Cake

This is a quick, easy and delicious chocolate cake. I made this for my friend Larry's birthday.

Cake:
2 cups sugar
2 cups flour
½ teaspoon salt
1 teaspoon cinnamon
2 sticks butter
1 cup water
4 tablespoons cocoa
2 large eggs
½ cup buttermilk
1 teaspoon vanilla
1 teaspoon baking soda

In a bowl, mix flour, sugar, salt and cinnamon and set aside. In a saucepan combine butter, water, and cocoa and bring to a boil. Set aside. In a large bowl, combine eggs, buttermilk, vanilla and soda. Add dry ingredients and cocoa mixture to buttermilk mixture until well combined. Pour into a greased 13 x 9-inch baking pan. Bake at 350° for 20-25 minutes.

Frosting:
1 stick butter
4 tablespoons cocoa
6 tablespoons milk
1 pound confectioner's sugar, sifted
1 teaspoon vanilla
1 cup chopped pecans, toasted

Bring butter, cocoa, and milk to a boil in a saucepan. Remove from heat. Add sugar and vanilla. Put back on low heat and beat until sugar has melted and there are not lumps. Pour over the warm cake.

The Inn at Blackberry Farm's Chocolate Buttermilk Cake with Black berry Meringue

Thanks so much to The Inn at Blackberry Farm and Chef John Fleer for allowing me to use this recipe. I LOVE this cake.

Chocolate Cake:
Vegetable oil spray
3 cups all purpose flour
2 cups granulated sugar
¾ cup unsweetened Dutch-process Cocoa powder
2 teaspoons baking soda
1 teaspoon salt
2-1/2 cups fresh or thawed frozen blackberries
1 cup low-fat (1.5%) buttermilk
2/3 cup vegetable oil
2 tablespoons distilled white vinegar
2 teaspoons pure vanilla extract

Blackberry Filling:
¾ cup egg whites (about 6)
1-1/2 cups granulated sugar
½ teaspoon cream of tartar
1-1/2 cups seedless blackberry preserves at room temperature
1 pint fresh or thawed blackberries plus additional berries for garnish
2 tablespoons confectioner's sugar

To Make the Chocolate Cake: Preheat oven to 350°. Coat two 9-by- 2-inch round pans with vegetable oil spray and line the bottoms with parchment paper. Lightly spray the paper. In a large bowl, sift together the flour, sugar, cocoa and baking soda and salt.

Pass the blackberries through a fine strainer set over a bowl; you should have 1 cup puree. Whisk in the buttermilk, oil, vinegar and vanilla. Pour the blackberry mixture into the dry ingredients. Divide the batter evenly between the prepared pans and bake for about 40 minutes, or until the cakes pull away from the sides and the tops spring back when pressed. Let cool on a rack for 10 minutes, then unmold and cool completely.

Make the Blackberry Filling: In a large heatproof bowl set over a saucepan of simmering water, whisk the egg whites with the granulated sugar and cream of tartar until the sugar dissolves and the whites are hot to the touch, about 5 minutes. Transfer to a standing mixer and beat at high speed until the meringue cools to room temperature and is very thick, about 15 minutes. Stir the blackberry preserves until smooth, then gently fold 1 cup into the meringue.

Using a serrated knife, split the cakes in half horizontally. Thinly spread the ½ cup of preserves on 3 of the cut cake layers. Set one of the layers on a large plate, preserves side up. Spread one-third of the meringue on top and press one-third of the blackberries into the meringue. Repeat with the 2 remaining preserves-spread cake layers and the remaining meringue and blackberries. Top with the final cake layer and let stand at room temperature for 1 to 3 hours. Just before serving, sift the confectioners' sugar over the top of the cake and garnish with the additional blackberries.

Make Ahead: The chocolate cake can be baked up to 1 day in advance and kept at room temperature.

Chocolate Mousse Cake

7 ounces semi-sweet chocolate
1 stick unsalted butter
7 eggs, separated
1 cup sugar
1 teaspoon vanilla extract
1/8 teaspoon cream of tartar
Whipped Cream Frosting (recipe follows)

Preheat oven to 325°. In a small saucepan, melt chocolate and butter over low heat.

In a large bowl, beat egg yolks and ¾ cup sugar until very light and fluffy, about 5 minutes. Gradually beat in warm chocolate mixture and vanilla.

In another large bowl, beat egg whites with cream of tartar until soft peaks form. Add remaining ¼ cup sugar, 1 tablespoon at a time. Continue beating until stiff. Fold egg whites carefully into chocolate mixture. Pour ¾ of the batter into an ungreased 9 x 3-inch spring form pan. Cover remaining batter and refrigerate. Bake cake for 35 minutes.

Prepare whipped cream frosting; set aside. Remove cake from oven and cool. Cake will drop as it cools. Remove outside ring of spring form pan. Stir refrigerated batter to soften slightly. Spread on top of cake. Refrigerate until firm. Spread whipped cream frosting over top and sides. Refrigerate several hours or overnight. Also may be frozen.

Whipped Cream Frosting: Whip ½ pt. whipping cream till soft peaks form. Add 1/3 cup confectioner's sugar and 1 teaspoon vanilla and whip until stiff. Serves 8.

Note: Do not eat this cake if worried about raw eggs.

Alpine Chocolate Pound Cake

1 box Swiss Chocolate Cake Mix
1 cup sour cream
1 cup milk
3 eggs
1 teaspoon vanilla
2/3 cup oil or melted butter
1 small box chocolate pudding

Preheat oven to 350°. Mix cake mix and all other ingredients in a large bowl with a wire whisk until thoroughly mixed. Bake in a 10-inch Bundt pan for 50-60 minutes or until a cake tester comes out clean.

Chocolate, Coconut Candy Cake

Cake:
1 stick plus 3 tablespoons butter
1-1/2 cups sugar
2 eggs
2 cups all-purpose flour
½ teaspoon soda
1-1/4 teaspoon baking powder
4 tablespoons cocoa
1 cup buttermilk
1 teaspoon vanilla

Cream butter and sugar, add eggs. Add dry ingredients alternating with buttermilk. Add vanilla. Place batter into two 9-inch greased and floured cake pans. Bake at 350° for 25 minutes or until a cake tester comes out clean when inserted into the center of the cake. Cool on clean dish towels and split into 4 layers with a sharp knife.

Coconut Filling:
1 cup evaporated milk
2 cups sweetened coconut
12 large marshmallows
1 cup sugar
1 cup chopped pecans

Place all ingredients in a saucepan and simmer for 5 minutes. Place between cake layers.

Frosting:
1/3 cup milk
¼ cup butter
1 (6-ounce) package chocolate chips
1 teaspoon vanilla
2-1/2 cups confectioners' sugar

Combine milk and butter. Bring to a boil. Remove from heat and add chocolate chips, vanilla and sugar. Blend well. Frost cake on top.

Toasted Coconut Cake

The best of all Southern cakes is the coconut cake. I created this one for a cheese company and it was in their national magazine. It's easy, and the ingredients will surprise you. Enjoy!

Cake:
1-1/2 sticks unsalted butter, room temperature
1-1/2 cups sugar
½ cup pineapple preserves
4 large eggs
3 cups self-rising flour
1 cup sour cream
1 teaspoon vanilla

Preheat oven to 325°. Grease and flour (I use a baking spray) 4 (9-inch) cake pans. With an electric mixer, beat the butter, sugar and pineapple preserves until light and fluffy. Add the eggs one at a time to the sugar mixture. Add alternately the flour, and sour cream, ending with the flour. Add the vanilla, and beat on high speed for 2 minutes. Add the batter evenly between the 4 pans. Bake for 20-25 minutes or until a cake tester comes out clean. Remove from the oven. After 10 minutes, remove the cakes from the pans to a rack to cool. Then frost with the icing below.
Note: To make cupcakes, use an ice cream scoop and place the batter into 2-1/2 inch cupcake cups. Bake for approximately 20 minutes or until done. Remove the cupcakes to a rack to cool.

Frosting:
1-1/2 sticks unsalted butter, softened
1-1/2 (8-ounce) containers Mascarpone cheese or 1-1/2 (8-ounce) packages cream cheese
1-1/2 pounds confectioner's sugar
3 teaspoon coconut extract
*1 (8-ounce) package coconut, toasted

Place the coconut on a cookie sheet and place in a 350° oven. Watch carefully and stir often until the coconut is lightly browned. Remove from the oven and set aside to cool.
Mix the butter, and mascarpone or cream cheese in a mixer with a wire whisk until creamy. Add the confectioner's sugar and the coconut extract. Mix until the sugar is well blended into the butter and cheese mixture. Spread the frosting between layers along with a little of the toasted coconut. Spread frosting on tops and sides of the cake. Using your hand like a cup, place the toasted coconut on the sides and top of the cake. Refrigerate. Bring the cake to room temperature before serving.
*I use the organic dried coconut available at Whole Foods. If this coconut is not available, just use Baker's Angel Flake coconut, and either toast it, or just use it like it is.

Coconut Rum Chocolate Cakes

I could not tell you on this day where I got this recipe, but it's good and I sold lots of these little cakes at the Farmers Market several years ago.

3 ounces bittersweet chocolate, chopped
½ stick unsalted butter
½ cup sugar
2 large eggs
2 tablespoons dark rum
½ teaspoon vanilla
½ teaspoon salt
1/3 cup flour
½ cup sweetened flaked coconut, toasted and cooled

Preheat oven to 350°. Butter and flour six ½ cup muffin tins.
In a metal bowl over simmering water melt the chocolate with the butter, whisking until smooth. Remove bowl from heat and whisk in sugar. Whisk in eggs one at a time, and add remaining ingredients, whisking until combined well. Divide batter among prepared tins and bake in the middle of oven until a tester comes out clean, 20-25 minutes. Turn out onto a wire rack to cool.

Mocha Ice Cream Cake

1 package ladyfingers or enough to line a 9-inch spring form pan
½ gallon coffee ice cream, softened
1 quart chocolate ice cream, softened
2 tablespoons instant coffee granules
½ cup coffee flavored liqueur
6 chocolate covered toffee bars, crushed
Chocolate sauce
1 cup heavy cream, whipped

Line ladyfingers around sides of 9-inch spring form pan. Mix ice creams together. Add coffee, liqueur and crushed toffee bars. Pour into pan. Spread a thin layer of chocolate sauce on top. Freeze. Before serving, spread cake with whipped cream. Do not let cake defrost before serving. Serves 8.

Cream Cheese Pound Cake

Just the best cake around. It has a "crust" like a pound cake should have. It' great to eat with fruit or berries in the summer, or just cut a slice and have a bite.

3 sticks butter, at room temperature
1 (8-ounce) package cream cheese, softened
3 cups sugar
6 large eggs
2 teaspoons vanilla extract
3 cups all-purpose flour
Pinch salt

Beat the butter and cream cheese until light and fluffy. Add the sugar and beat again until sugar is mixed in well. Add eggs one at a time, beating until yellow disappears. Add vanilla. Add flour and salt gradually to the creamed mixture.

Pour the batter into a greased and floured 10-inch tube pan. Bake at 300° for 1 hour and 30 minutes or until a cake tester comes out clean. Let cool in the pan for 10 minutes. Remove from pan onto a wire rack to cool.

Mother's Hummingbird Cake (1)

3 cups all-purpose flour
2 cups sugar
1 teaspoon cinnamon
1 teaspoon baking soda
1/2 teaspoon salt
8 ounces crushed pineapple with juice
3 large eggs, well beaten
2 cups chopped banana
2 cups chopped pecans, toasted
1-1/2 teaspoons vanilla
1 cup vegetable oil
1 teaspoon butter, melted
1 cup confectioner's sugar

Preheat oven to 325°. Generously grease and flour (use Baker's Joy or Pam Baking Spray) a 10-inch tube or Bundt pan. In a large bowl, stir together the flour, sugar, cinnamon, baking soda and salt. Remove 2 tablespoons pineapple juice and set aside for later use in the glaze.

Add the crushed pineapple, oil, eggs, bananas, nuts and vanilla to the flour mixture and stir until just blended. Do not beat.

Pour the batter into the prepared pan. Bake about 1 hour and 10 minutes or until a wooden pick comes out clean. Cool in the pan for 15 minutes then invert on a wire rack, remove the pan and cool completely.

In a small mixing bowl, combine the melted butter, confectioner's sugar and reserved pineapple juice. Make a smooth glaze and pour around top of cake.

Mother's Hummingbird Layer Cake with Cream Cheese Icing (2)

Cake:
3 cups all-purpose flour
2 cups sugar
1 teaspoon salt
1 teaspoon cinnamon
1 teaspoon baking soda
3 eggs, beaten
1-1/2 cups vegetable oil
1-1/2 teaspoons vanilla
1 (8-ounce) can pineapple, undrained
2 cups chopped toasted pecans, divided
2 cups chopped banana

Icing:
1 (8-ounce) package cream cheese, softened
1 stick butter, softened
1 (16-ounce) powdered sugar
1 teaspoon vanilla
1 cup chopped pecans

Combine dry ingredients in a large mixing bowl. Add eggs, and oil and stir until all ingredients are moistened. Do not beat. Stir in the vanilla, pineapple, and 1 cup of chopped pecans and the banana. Spoon into 3 well-greased and floured 9-inch cake pans. Bake in a preheated 350° oven for 25-30 minutes or until a cake tester inserted in the center of the cake comes out clean. Cool in the pans for 10 minutes and then remove cake from the pans and cool on wire racks before icing.
For icing: In a large bowl of an electric mixer with a whisk attachment, whip butter and cream cheese until light and fluffy. Add the powdered sugar, vanilla and nuts. Ice the cake between layers and on tops and side.

Mommy's Lemon Cheese Cake & Lemon Cheese Cake Icing

My mother e-mailed me my grandmother, Mommy's recipe back in 2003 after I had asked her for it. I could not remember my grandmother making this cake, but mother and my cousin Sandra said that during the early years, she made it all the time. In the South we called it Lemon Cheese Cake and sometimes, Lemon Jelly Cake. I'm happy to pass my grandmother's recipe on to you.

Cake:
1 cup butter (2 sticks)
2 cups sugar
1 tablespoon baking powder (this is what my mother wrote!)
3 cups sifted cake flour
¾ cup milk
6 egg whites, stiffly beaten
1-1/2 teaspoons vanilla

Cream the butter and sugar with mixer, beating until light and fluffy. Add the sifted dry ingredients alternating with the milk. Fold in the egg whites. Pour into 3 greased and floured 8-inch cake pans. Bake in a 350° oven for 25-30 minutes or until top springs back when lightly touched. Cool on racks.

Lemon Cheese Filling:
½ cup butter
1 cup sugar
6 egg yolks
Grated rind of 2 lemons
Juice of 2 lemons

Combine all ingredients in top of double boiler. Cook over hot water, stirring constantly until thick. Strain to remove any cooked egg whites. Cool. Place between and on top of cooled cake.

Lemon Cheese Cake Filling
Also known as Lemon Jelly Cake Filling

This is my grandmother Irene's "filling." Use the recipe for Coconut Cake and ice it with the lemon cheese filling below instead of the Coconut Cream Cheese Icing. Make 2 recipes of the filling for a 4 layer cake.

1 cup sugar
2-1/2 tablespoons flour
1 teaspoon butter
¼ cup lemon juice
1 egg
Grated zest of 2 lemons

Mix dry ingredients. Add the egg, slightly beaten; add butter, lemon juice, and rind. Stirring constantly, cook over medium heat until thickened. Strain to remove any "scrambled egg." Cool. Spread on layers and top of cake.
Note: Double this recipe for 2 layers.

Lemonade Cake

Cake:
1 box Lemon cake mix
1 small can lemonade mix-divided into 3$^{rds.}$
3 eggs
1/3 cup oil
1 teaspoon butter extract
1 (8-ounce) pkg. Cream cheese
1 stick butter
1 pound confectioner's sugar

Put cake mix in mixer. Add 3 eggs. Pour 1/3 of lemonade mix into a measuring cup. Add enough water to make 1-1/4 cups. Add to mixing bowl. Add 1/3 cup of oil, and 1 teaspoon butter extract. Beat for 30 seconds, on low then 2 minutes on medium. Place the batter into two well greased (spray with Baker's Joy) 9-inch baking pans. Bake for about 25-30 minutes on 325°. Remove when done. Cool on racks.

Icing: Beat softened cream cheese and butter together. Add 1 pound of sifted confectioner's sugar. Add another 1/3 of the lemonade mix from the can. (Do not use the last 1/3 cup yet).

Heat the remaining 1/3 cup of lemonade mix. Place one cake layer on a cake plate. Punch holes in cake layer with a fork. Pour the lemonade mix over the cake with a spoon. Frost the cake layer with cream cheese icing. Place the second layer over the first, and repeat with the lemonade, and cream cheese icing. Frost the top and sides of cake with the cream cheese icing.

Lucky Lemon Cake

My friend Nell Redfern who now lives in Gilmer, Texas gave me some wonderful cake recipes. This is one of them. Thanks, Nell.

2 (3-ounce) packages ladyfingers
2 (14-ounce) cans sweetened condensed milk
8 eggs, separated
2 teaspoons lemon zest
14-15 tablespoons lemon juice
¼ teaspoon cream of tartar
Powdered sugar
1 thin slice lemon for garnish

Preheat the oven to 375°. Lightly grease or spray a 9 x 3-inch spring form pan. Cover bottom of the pan with ladyfingers, cutting to fit. Stand remaining ladyfingers around sides of pan, cutting bottoms so that tops are even with the pan, otherwise the tops will burn. In a large bowl, mix condensed milk, egg yolks, lemon peel and lemon juice. In a medium bowl, beat egg whites with cream of tartar until stiff. Fold into first mixture. Pour batter into prepared pan. Bake 25 minutes or until top is lightly browned. Cool completely. At this point you can cover with foil, place in a plastic bag and freeze up to 3 months.

If serving the same day, remove the outside ring of pan, place the lemon with a twist in the center, and dust with confectioner's sugar. Let stand at room temperature for 15 minutes before serving. Serves 12.

Keep covered in the refrigerator.

Key Lime Cake

I got this recipe via e-mail from my mother in September of 2002. She sent the recipe and a note that said, "You just have to make this." So, I will share it with you too!

1 (18.25 ounce) package lemon cake mix
1 (3-ounce) package instant lemon pudding mix
½ cup water
¾ cup vegetable oil
4 eggs
5 tablespoons key lime juice

Glaze:
1-1/2 cups confectioners' sugar
3 tablespoons lime juice

Mix together and pour on warm cake.

Preheat oven to 350°. Lightly grease a *13 X 9-inch glass baking dish, or a 10-inch Bundt pan. In a large bowl, mix together the lemon cake mix, lemon instant pudding, water, oil, eggs, and 5 table-spoons lime juice. Mix well. Pour into the cake pan. Bake for 45 minutes* or until a toothpick comes out clean in the center. *Watch the time if using a shallow pan. It may cook faster. Remove from oven and if using a Bundt pan, cool for 15 minutes before turning out to cool on a wire rack.
After the cake cools, pour on the glaze.

Fresh Peach Cake

Cake:
2 cups all-purpose flour
5 tablespoon plus 1 teaspoon cornstarch
2 teaspoons baking powder
½ teaspoon salt
1-1/2 stick butter, softened
1-1/3 cups sugar
¾ cup milk
2 teaspoons vanilla extract
9 large egg whites, stiffly beaten

Cream Filling:
2 cups heavy cream
½ cup sugar
2 teaspoons vanilla extract

Peach Filling:
6 large peaches
½ teaspoon almond extract
Juice of ½ lemon
3 tablespoons sugar

Cream filling: Make the cream filling by mixing the cream, sugar and vanilla and placing in the fridge until the cake has cooled. Whip the cream just before assembling the cake.
Preheat the oven to 350°.
Cake: Grease and flour three 8-inch cake pans. Line the bottom of the pans with parchment and grease and flour the parchment. Set aside.
Mix the flour, cornstarch, salt and baking powder together in a small bowl.
In a mixing bowl, cream the butter, and sugar together until light and fluffy. Add the dry mixture, alternating with the milk, ending with the flour. Add the vanilla. Mix well.
Fold the beaten egg whites into the batter, being careful not to deflate the eggs, but mixing well.
Divide batter among the cake pans. Bake for 20-25 minutes or until a cake tester inserted in the cake comes out clean. Let cakes cool for 10 minutes before removing from the pan. Cool on racks before icing.
Peach Filling: Peel peaches, and slice. Place the peaches in the lemon juice, almond extract and sugar.
Place one cake layer on a cake plate or pedestal. Pour some of the juice from the peaches over the cake layer, and let it soak in. Place a third of the peach slices on the bottom of the cake layer. Cover with

part of the whipped cream. Repeat cake, peach juice, peaches, and whipped cream, until all three layers have been covered in peaches and cream. Use long skewers to hold cake together if it starts to slide. Keep refrigerated.

Maple Pecan Torte

Torte:
¾ cup light brown sugar
4 egg yolks
1-1/3 cups ground pecans
1 tablespoon dried white bread crumbs
1 tablespoon strong coffee
3 egg whites

Filling:
1-1/4 cups whipping cream
1 tablespoon strong coffee
3-4 tablespoons maple syrup

Decoration:
2 (1-ounce) squares semi-sweet chocolate, melted
8 rose leaves

Preheat oven to 350°. Grease and line a deep 8-inch round cake pan with waxed paper. In a bowl, whisk sugar and egg yolks until thick and light. Gently fold in ground nuts and bread crumbs, and then stir in the coffee. In a bowl, whisk egg whites until soft peaks form. Fold into mixture. Pour into prepared pan and bake in oven 25-30 minutes, until well risen and firm to touch. Turn onto a wire rack to cool.
To make chocolate leaves, brush chocolate over underside of rose leaves. Place on waxed paper and let stand until completely set. Peel off leaves.
To make the filling, in a bowl, whip cream and coffee until thick. Stir in maple syrup. Slice cooled cake horizontally in 2 layers and sandwich together with ½ of the cream. Spread remaining cream over cake and decorate with the chocolate leaves. 8 servings.

Sour Cream Pound Cake

My cousin Joyce Kimbrough in Tuscumbia, Alabama has been making this recipe for 45 years or more. The recipe was left in her milk box on a flyer from the State of Alabama Department of Agriculture & Industries in Montgomery. A.W. Todd was the commissioner at the time.

2 sticks butter or margarine
1/2 teaspoon lemon flavoring
1 teaspoon vanilla flavoring
¼ teaspoon almond flavoring
3 cups sugar
6 eggs
3 cups flour, sifted
1/4 teaspoon soda
1/2 teaspoon salt
8 ounces sour cream

Cream butter and add sugar one cup at a time. Add eggs, one at a time
mixing well after each. Add flavorings. Sift together flour, soda and
salt. Add flour mixture and sour cream to butter mixture, alternating each.
Beat well. Place in 10-inch greased and floured tube pan and bake at 350° about one hour.

Tiramisu Cake

Cake:
3 eggs
½ cup plus 1 tablespoon sugar
¾ cup all-purpose flour
1 tablespoon instant coffee granules, if desired

Filling:
12 ounces mascarpone cheese
4 egg yolks
½ cup sugar
2 tablespoons dark rum
2 egg whites

Finish:
¾ cup coffee
2 (1-ounce) squares semi-sweet chocolate, grated

To make the cake, preheat the oven to 350°. Grease and line a deep 8-inch round cake pan with waxed paper. In a bowl, whisk eggs and sugar until light and thick. Sift flour and coffee granules over mixture, and fold in gently. Spoon mixture into a prepared pan and bake in the oven for 30 minutes, or until cake is golden and springs back when pressed in the center. Turn onto a wire rack to cool.
To make the filling, in a bowl, beat the mascarpone until soft. In another bowl, whisk the egg yolks and sugar until light and thick. Stir in the mascarpone and rum. In a clean bowl, whisk the egg whites until soft peaks form; fold into the cheese mixture.
Cut the cake horizontally in 3 layers. Put 1 layer on a serving plate. Sprinkle with 1/3 of coffee. Cover with 1/3 of filling. Repeat layers, finishing with a topping of cheese mixture. Chill overnight. Sprinkle with grated chocolate to serve. Makes 8 servings.
Note: Don't use this recipe if you are worried about using raw eggs.

Victoria Cake

This is one of my favorite cakes for tea time. Named after Queen Victoria who loved tea time, this cake can be made and filled with any jam or curd. It's simple and delicious.

When I serve this cake, I put it on a cake pedestal and cover it with a pretty tea towel.

1 cup unsalted butter, softened
1 cup sugar
4 large eggs, beaten
2 cups self-rising flour

Strawberry, raspberry, blackberry, apricot jam or lemon curd make great fillings.
Choose one!

Preheat the oven to 375°. Spray two (7or 8-inch) pans with baking spray. Cream the butter and sugar with a wooden spoon or a mixer until light and fluffy. Add the beaten eggs gradually, making sure the eggs are well mixed into the butter sugar mixture. Gradually add the flour, mixing thoroughly. Divide the mixture between the pans. Bake for 20-25 minutes or until a cake tester comes out clean. Cool for 10 minutes in the pan. Remove to a wire rack to cool.

Place jam or curd between layers and sprinkle the top with sugar.

Cookies & Candy

Baked Chocolate Covered Cherry Cookies

I have always loved chocolate covered cherries. So these cookies are one of my favorites from mother.

Cookies:
1 stick butter
1 cup sugar
1 egg
1-1/2 teaspoon vanilla
1-1/2 cups flour
½ cup unsweetened cocoa powder
¼ teaspoon baking powder
¼ teaspoon baking soda
10-ounce jar maraschino cherries—drained but save the juice

Frosting:
1 cup (6-ounce package) semi-sweet chocolate chips
½ cup sweetened condensed milk
1-1/2 teaspoons maraschino cherry juice

Cookies: Cream butter, sugar, egg and vanilla until light and fluffy. Add flour, cocoa, baking powder and baking soda. Mix at low speed until a stiff dough forms, (about 1 minute). Shape dough into 1-inch balls and place 2-inches apart on ungreased cookie sheets. Push a cherry into each ball. When all cookies are ready, prepare frosting as follows.

Frosting: In a small saucepan over low heat, melt chocolate chips with condensed milk, stirring constantly. Remove from heat and add 1-1/2 teaspoons cherry juice. Frost each ball with ½ teaspoon frosting. Bake at 350° for 8-10 minutes until puffy. Store tightly covered. Makes 36-48 cookies.

Chocolate Covered Blueberries!

I love these! I had some leftover chocolate coating for strawberries and there were blueberries in the fridge at the same time, so I decided to use them too. I never realized how good chocolate and blueberries could be together until I made these.

1 (7-ounce) container semi sweet Bakers Dipping Chocolate
1/2 pint blueberries, washed and *completely dried

Melt chocolate in the microwave according to package directions.* Make sure that blueberries are completely dry, otherwise the chocolate will seize.
Place the blueberries in the chocolate by the tablespoons, mix, and remove with a fork. Place the chocolate-covered blueberries on parchment paper to dry. Refrigerate.

Chocolate Nut Toffee Bars

1 cup butter, softened
1 cup confectioner's sugar
1-1/4 cups flour
1/3 cup cocoa
1 (14-ounce) can sweetened condensed milk
2 teaspoon vanilla extract
1 cup semi-sweet chocolate chips
¾ cup chopped pecans, or almonds, toasted

Preheat oven to 350°. Reserve 2 tablespoons butter. In a large mixing bowl beat remaining butter, and sugar until fluffy. Add flour and cocoa and mix well. With floured hands, press into a greased 13 X 9-inch baking pan. Bake for 15 minutes.
In a medium saucepan combine the 2 tablespoons reserved butter, sweetened condensed milk and cook and stir until mixture thickens slightly, about 15 minutes. Remove from heat, stir in vanilla. Pour over the crust. Bake 10-15 minutes longer or until golden brown. Remove from the oven and immediately sprinkle the chocolate chips over the topping. Let stand for 1 minute. Spread the chips while warm. Top with the toasted nuts. Cut into diamonds. 24-36 bars.

Little Devils

12 ounces of Chocolate Kisses or 2 (6-ounce) packages of chocolate chips
½ cup crunchy peanut butter
5 cups Corn flakes

Melt the kisses. Add the peanut butter. Add enough corn flakes for the chocolate kisses to coat. Spoon on to a cookie sheet lined with parchment or waxed paper.

French Creams

I made this recipe on CBS-7 with Judy Booker and Heather Sullivan, just a couple of days before Christmas this year.

2 small packages semi-sweet chocolate chips (12-ounces)
1 can sweetened condensed milk (fat-free if you like)
1 teaspoons vanilla extract
1 cup chopped pecans, toasted
1-1/2 cups coconut or ½ cup Italian cocoa

Melt chocolate chips over hot water. Stir in milk, vanilla and 1 cup nuts. Chill. Roll into ball by teaspoonfuls with buttered hands. Roll in coconut and/or Italian cocoa.

Parisian Sweets

1 pound dates
1 pound dried figs
1 pound nuts, toasted
Confectioner's sugar

Pull stems from figs. Mix fruit and nuts and force through a meat chopper. Knead on a board dredged in confectioner's sugar. Roll ¼" thick and form small balls. Roll in confectioner's sugar. Pack in layers in a tin box and layer between sheets of wax paper.

Southern Candy Clusters

8 ounces semi-sweet chocolate
½ cup salted, roasted peanuts, or pecans, toasted
½ cup seedless raisins
Miniature marshmallows (optional)

Line 2 baking sheets with parchment paper. In the top of a double boiler set over hot water, melt the chocolate, stirring constantly until smooth.

Remove the double boiler from the heat, keeping the chocolate warm over the hot water. (Do not let chocolate and water meet! Otherwise you will have a GLOB of chocolate because the chocolate will seize.) Stir the peanuts (or pecans) and raisins into the chocolate, coating them with chocolate. Drop by tablespoons onto the parchment paper, spacing them 1-inch apart. Let the clusters stand at room temperature until firm. This may take several hours. Store the clusters in an airtight container.

Le Cordon Bleu Truffles

(As I made them at LCB using kitchen scales)

200 ml Crème
250 G Chocolat Mi-Amer
30 ml Alcool De Poires, ou autres
Finition
100 G Chocolat Mi-Amer
50 G Cacao

Translation-
180 grams heavy cream
250 G Bittersweet Chocolate, chopped
30 ml Pear liqueur, rum, cognac, Grand Marnier
Finish:
100 G Bittersweet chocolate, melted
50 G Cocoa

Put the cream on to boil. Put a touch of vanilla in the cream. Put the chopped chocolate in a double boiler and add the boiling cream. Mix well with a whisk. Put alcohol in at this stage. Mix until the chocolate is melted. Do not beat. When the chocolate is cold, roll into a ball. Coat with the melted 100 G of Bittersweet chocolate that has been melted, gotten cold again and then re-melted. Then roll in cocoa. After the truffles get hard, roll in a sifter to remove any excess cocoa.
Note: The truffles can be made ahead and put in the refrigerator for the next day, but you must bring them to room temperature to finish them. We also had to place the warm chocolate on marble, then put the chocolate back in the bowl and warm again. This is called "tempering."

Lemon Raisin Cookie Bars

I love these little cookie bars. Ummm—the most delicious little things!

Crust:
2 cups all-purpose flour
1/2 cup sugar
2/3 cup butter

Mix the above ingredients until crumbly and press into a 13 x 9-inch baking pan.
Bake in a preheated 350° oven for 15-20 minutes or until light brown.

Filling:
4 eggs
2 cups sugar
4 tablespoons all-purpose flour
1 teaspoon baking powder
1/2 teaspoon salt
2 tablespoons orange zest
4 tablespoons orange juice
1-1/2 cups raisins, chopped
1 cup sweetened flaked coconut

Combine eggs and next 8 ingredients and pour over the baked crust. Bake at 350° for 20-30 minutes or until set.

Topping:
4 teaspoons orange juice
4 teaspoons lemon juice
3 teaspoons butter, softened
2 cups sifted confectioner's sugar

Combine the above ingredients and beat it with an electric mixer until smooth. Pour the topping mixture over the hot layer. Cool on a wire rack. Cut into bars.
May be frozen for up to 3 months. Make about 3 dozen small bars.

Chewy Chocolate, Chocolate Chip Cookies

This recipe came from my secretary, Jennifer in Orlando, FL. Jennifer liked to cook and she brought these for me one morning, along with the recipe. She made gooood cookies!

1 cup butter, softened
¼ cup shortening
2 eggs
2 tablespoons vanilla
2 cups flour
¼ teaspoon salt
1 teaspoon baking powder
¾ cup cocoa powder
1 cup sugar
1 cup brown sugar, packed
1 cup semi-sweet chocolate chips

Preheat the oven to 350°. Mix together the butter, shortening and sugars. Add eggs and vanilla and beat on high speed with a mixer until mixture is light and fluffy. With a spoon, mix in flour, and the remaining ingredients including the chocolate chips. Let stand for 3-5 minutes.
Line a cookie sheet with parchment. Drop dough onto cookie sheet by tablespoons, about 3 inches apart. Bake for 8-10 minutes. Remove from the oven. Let the cookies rest of the cookie sheet for a couple of minutes to set slightly before removing to a wire rack to cool.

Rugelach

I remember the first time I had rugelach in south Florida. Everyone was making a big deal over having it. I have to admit that I'd never heard of it before and didn't know what to expect. It was a delicious little treat.

The original recipe is from McMead's in Miami.

1 pound of butter, softened
1 pint sour cream
2 tablespoons sugar
4 cups flour, sifted
1 (16-ounce) jar apricot jam
½ cup coconut
½ cup walnuts
½ cup raisins

Cream the butter, sour cream and sugar and then add in the flour. Chill for several hours. Then remove the dough from the refrigerator and roll one third of it into an 8 x 20 inch rectangle. Spread a third of the jam, coconut, walnuts and raisins over half the dough (lengthwise). Fold the dough over and cut it into 2 by 4-inch rectangles. Sprinkle them with sugar and bake in a preheated 350° oven for 40 minutes. Repeat with remaining two thirds, rolled out in the same size segments, or freeze as much dough as you like before rolling it out.

Pies & Tarts

Mama Irene's Secret Pie Recipe

I came home from the book club meeting late and tired. While I was putting a leftover bottle of wine in the refrigerator, I saw a bottle of Coke behind the milk. I took it out, and it was icy cold.

Even though it was late, and I knew it would keep me awake, I drank it. And, I stepped back in time to the 1950s when my grandmother's old refrigerator always had a lightly capped bottle of Coca-Cola just waiting for me to enjoy.

There's nothing like it in the world when you want something a little cold and a little sweet.

That old refrigerator held a lot of good food. In it were eggs from my grandmother's chickens (and sometimes chicken from my grandmother's chickens). In the summer there were peas from Mrs. Daniel's garden, and fresh perch from Mrs. Kirkham's pond. That's the way life was back then.

There was not much eaten from a can, and the nearest restaurant was miles away, so there was no way to eat out.

My grandmother had a cow, so there was fresh milk and cream in the refrigerator, too. I still remember how she churned her own butter. Once, when my grandmother was milking her cow, the cow kicked her and granddaddy asked her to please get rid of the cow and buy milk from the store.

"No," she said adamantly.

She continued on milking the cow for as long as she could.

The churn that she used back in those days is in my own kitchen full of rolling pins. I cherish it to this day.

I think that my grandmother loved being a farm wife. It was only a small farm, but it provided everything that was needed to comfortably exist in the world that my grandparents lived in. The only complaint that I ever heard my grandmother make is that she wanted a more modern kitchen. Other than that, I think that life might have been just the way she wanted it to be—simple and uncomplicated.

It's funny: These days, we are all looking for what she had back then.

My grandmother was an educated woman. She met my grandfather while he was attending Auburn and she was a teacher. In a newspaper article that I found some years ago, it quotes my grandfather as saying, "I knew that I was going to marry that girl as soon as I met her."

But it would be a few years after he met her, because after he finished at Auburn, he went away again to a college out west.

My grandmother was a great cook. She made wonderful chicken pie, and chicken and dressing, and the best-fried chicken I've ever had. Her secret to fried chicken was soaking it in what we would call brine today—cold, salty water.

First, she would have someone kill the chicken and feather it. She would cut the chicken up, wash it and then soak it in the cold salted water in the refrigerator. When the chicken had soaked, she rinsed it, dipped it in self-rising seasoned flour and fried it in a hot iron skillet.

It was incredible and no small task to have chicken back in those days.

I think my grandmother was most famous for her chocolate pie. It was a recipe that she really didn't want to share. When the local paper featured her in a fairly large article, she reluctantly gave them her recipe for the chocolate pie. Her friends kept calling and telling her that the pie they made from her recipe did not taste as good as hers.

After reviewing the recipe that she gave the paper, we discovered that she had said one tablespoon of salt where it should have said one teaspoon of salt.

I have modified it to even less.

Sacred as it is, I am going to give you the secret recipe. My children think it's the best chocolate pie they have ever had. Let me know what you think.

With love, here's my grandmother's pie recipe.

A taste from the past:

Mama Irene's Secret Chocolate Pie

My son Rob's Favorite-chocolate pie!

1 baked 9-inch pie shell
½ cup cocoa
1 cup sugar
¼ cup cornstarch
3 egg yolks (reserve whites for meringue)
¼ teaspoon salt
2 cups milk
1 teaspoon vanilla

Mix cocoa, sugar, cornstarch and salt. Add the unbeaten egg yolks with the milk and add to the dry mixture. Cook until thick, stirring constantly. Remove from heat and add vanilla. Pour into a baked pie crust, and top with meringue (see below). Bake for about 25 minutes at 325° degrees to cook the meringue.

To make meringue: beat the three reserved egg whites with a half teaspoon of baking powder. When the eggs are frothy, gradually add six tablespoons of sugar. Beat until stiff peaks form.

Rich Short Crust

1-1/2 cups all purpose flour (11 grams of protein per cup)
¼ teaspoon salt
1-1/2 sticks cold butter
5 tablespoons cold water (use 4 tablespoon of cold water for 12 grams protein per cup in the flour)

Place the first two ingredients in a food processor. Pulse a few times to mix. Cut the butter into ½ inch pieces. Place the butter on top of the flour and pulse 5 times. Add 5 tablespoons of the water and pulse 5-6 times. Test by picking up a small amount of the flour mixture and if it compresses, then it's ready. If not ready, pulse 1 to 3 more times. Remove dough when it compresses in your hand. Compress the dough into balls. Smear the balls with the heal of your hand to finish combining the butter and flour. Scrape the dough up and form into a disc. Wrap in plastic wrap. Refrigerate about 25 minutes or until ready to use.

Pâte Brisée

(Pie Crust)
1-3/4 cups all purpose flour
1 stick unsalted butter, cut into small pieces
2 tablespoon sugar
¼ teaspoon salt
1 tablespoon lemon juice
1 egg yolk, beaten
2 tablespoons ice water

Preheat oven to 425°. Place flour and butter in a food processor. Process on the "on" and "off" for about 8 times. Combine the salt, sugar, lemon juice, egg yolk and water in a small bowl. Turn on processor and add the liquid down the processor tube. Process until dough forms a ball. Chill the dough for 1 hour.

Roll the dough to 1/8-inch thickness on a floured surface. Fit into a 9-inc tart pan. Place parchment paper or wax paper inside the shell. Fill with beans or rice. Bake for 8 minutes. Reduce the oven temperature to 375°. Remove the parchment along with the filler. Place tart shell back in the oven and bake until golden brown. Remove from the oven and cool before using.

Almond Tiny Tarts

Almond Tart Filling:
¾ cup sugar
¾ cup heavy cream
1 teaspoon Amaretto
½ teaspoon almond extract
1 cup blanched sliced almonds
Apricot jam (optional)

Pastry dough:
1 cup + 2 tablespoons all-purpose flour
1 tablespoon sugar
¾ teaspoon salt
¼ teaspoon lemon zest
¼ teaspoon ground ginger
Pinch cinnamon
1 stick cold butter cut into small cubes
1 egg yolk
1 tablespoon water
½ teaspoon vanilla

To make the pastry: In a food processor combine the flour, sugar, salt, zest, ginger and cinnamon and pulse several times until blended. Place the butter cubes into the processor and pulse until the mixture resemble coarse cornmeal.

In a small bowl, combine the egg yolk, water and vanilla and whisk until well blended. Pour the egg mixture into the food processor through the chute and pulse until the dough comes together. Remove the dough from the processor and press into two disks, wrap in plastic wrap and refrigerate for at least 30 minutes.

Almond filling: In a medium saucepan, combine sugar, heavy cream, amaretto and almond extract, and blend well. Bring the mixture to a roaring boil, stirring constantly. Remove the mixture from the heat, stir in the almonds and set aside.

Preheat the oven to 350°. Have 16 ungreased 1-1/2 inch tartlet pans on a baking sheet. Turn the dough out onto a floured surface and roll each disk out to a thickness of 3/8- inch, and cut into 16 circles that are 2-inches round. Press each circle into a tartlet pan. Place the tartlet pans on the rack in the center of the oven. Bake for 15 minutes. Remove from the oven and set aside. Increase the oven temperature to 400°. Fill each tartlet shell with a tablespoon of filling. Bake for 20 minutes or until the top is slightly caramel colored. They will continue to cook a more after you remove them from the oven. Cool on wire rack for 5 minutes or until set before removing the tartlet from the tartlet mold.

Note: If you would like to add another dimension of flavor, heat apricot jam and place a small amount on top of tart before serving.

Simple Fruit Tarts

9-inch Cookie pie shell in frozen food section Or Pâte Brisée
Blackberries
Blueberries
Raspberries
Sliced kiwi
½ cup seedless raspberry jam
½ cup good apricot preserves or jams

Thaw the dough and place the cookie dough in a 9-inch tart shell. Cut off any excess dough from the edges. Or make Pâte Brisée from above. Put foil or parchment paper in the shell and then fill the shell with rice or dried beans. Bake for 10 minutes in a 375°° preheated oven. Remove the paper and bean or rice and prick the shell all over with a fork. Bake for another 8 to 10 minutes or until the shell has browned. Set aside to cool.

Melt the raspberry jam in a small saucepan or the microwave. Place the raspberry jam on the bottom of the cooled tart shell. Fill the shell with fruit. Place the fruit on top of the raspberry jam. Melt the apricot jam and brush it on the fruit. Refrigerate any un-served tart.

Apple Pie

1-15 ounce package pie crust from refrigerator section
8 cups sliced, peeled apples
1 cup sugar
2 tablespoon flour
1 teaspoon cinnamon
1/8 teaspoon nutmeg
Dash of salt
1 tablespoon lemon juice

Preheat oven to 400° degrees. Place pie crust in a 9-inch or 10-inch deep dish pie pan. In a large bowl add the apples, sugar, flour, spices and lemon juice. Pour onto the pie crust. Place the second pie crust over the top and crimp. Cut a few vents in the top of the pie crust. Place on a parchment or foil lined baking sheet and bake for 55-70 minutes or until pie is bubbly and apples are tender. If crust starts to get too brown, cover the edges with foil.
Note: Sometimes I pour a little jarred caramel sauce into the vents before it gets done.

Black Cherry Pie

This came in an e-mail from mother. She said it was delicious. It was!

1 (14-ounce can condensed milk
1 cup heavy cream
2 lemons, juiced
1 cup chopped pecans, toasted
1 (16.5 ounce) can pitted Bing cherries, drained
1 (9-inch) prepared Graham cracker or Vanilla wafer pie crust

In a large bowl, combine condensed milk, lemon juice, pecans, and cherries.
In another bowl, whip heavy cream until soft peaks form.
Fold the milk mixture and heavy cream together. Pour into a pie crust and chill for at least 4 hours or until ready to serve.

Mother's Brown Sugar Coconut Pie

I have a note from my mother telling me that this pie is just delicious.

2 tablespoons brown sugar
2 tablespoons white sugar
3 tablespoons butter, softened
Dash salt
2 eggs, lightly beaten
1 (12-ounce) jar Butterscotch ice cream topping
1 teaspoon vanilla
1/2 cup coconut
1/2 cup chopped pecans, toasted
1 (9-inch) pie crust, unbaked

Pre-heat the oven to 350°. Combine all ingredients, stirring well after each addition. Pour into the pie shell. Bake for 40-45 minutes. Serve at room temperature.

Coconut Chocolate Chip Cookie Pie

1 (15-18 ounce) package Coconut chocolate chip cookies (low-fat cookies work just great too)
1 cup milk
1 (9-inch) pre-prepared Oreo pie crust
1 (12-ounce) container Cool Whip or Cool Whip Free

Dip 8 cookies in milk, and place in a single layer on the crust. Place one-third of the cool whip on top of the cookies. Make another layer of cookies and another layer of cool whip. The third layer of cookies will be the last, so put the cool whip on and crumble a few cookies on top of the cool whip. Top with a cherry.

Lemon Chess Tarts with Coconut whipped Cream and Toasted Coconut Topping

12 (3-inch) tart or pastry shells (found in the freezer section of the grocery store), blind baked according to package directions
5 eggs
1-1/4 cups sugar
3 tablespoons flour
¼ cup milk
½ cup lemon juice
Grated zest of 2 lemons
3 tablespoons unsalted butter, melted

Preheat the oven to 350°. With an electric mixer or with a wire whisk, beat together the eggs and the sugar in a medium bowl until combined. (Mixture should not be fluffy). Add the flour, milk, lemon juice, lemon zest and melted butter beating a few seconds between additions. Continue to beat for 5 minutes at medium speed. Pour the filling into the partially baked tart shells. Bake until the filling is barely firm and light golden brown on top, 30 minutes. Cool before serving.
Note: Depending on tart size, may not make all 12 tarts. Freeze the tarts that you don't serve, or keep refrigerated for dessert during the week.

Coconut Whipped Cream

1/2 cup heavy cream
2 tablespoons sugar
1/2 teaspoon coconut extract

Whip the cream until frothy. Add the sugar and coconut extract. Whip until soft peaks form.
Place a generous spoonful on top of the lemon tarts.

Toasted Coconut Topping: Toast 1/2 cup coconut in a 350° oven until light brown. Stir often to keep from over-browning. Cool before sprinkling over whipped cream.

Old-Fashioned Lemon Ice Box Pie with a Twist!

2 (9-inch) graham cracker or vanilla wafer pie crust
1 (6-ounce) can lemonade concentrate, thawed and undiluted
1 (14-ounce) can fat-free sweetened condensed milk
1 (8-ounce) container "free" frozen whipped topping, thawed
Lemon slices

Fold condensed milk and lemonade concentrate into the whipped topping; spoon evenly into crusts. Cover and freeze pies until firm. Garnish, if desired, before serving. Serves 12.

Lemon Ice Box Pie

This is my all-time favorite pie. I can't pass it up if I see it on a menu. I've been eating pie from this recipe as long as I can remember!

1-(10-inch deep dish) glass pie plate
1 box vanilla wafers
6 egg yolks
2 cans Fat-free Sweetened Condensed milk
1 cup lemon juice
1 (8-ounce) carton frozen "Free" whipped topping, make meringue if you like
Or 1 cup heavy cream whipped with 2 tablespoons sugar to soft peaks.

Preheat the oven to 325°. Line a deep dish pie plate with vanilla wafers on the bottom and coming up around the sides of the plate. In a mixer, combine the egg yolks, lemon juice and sweetened condensed milk. Mix well. Pour into the vanilla wafer crust and bake for 40 minutes. Remove from the oven to cool. Chill. Before serving, cover the pie with whipped topping.
Note: Cut this recipe in half if using a shallow pre-made pie crust. Buy or make two crusts and make two pies.

Peanut Butter Pie

1 cup confectioner's sugar
1 cup peanut butter, plain or crunchy
1 (8-ounce) package "1/3 less fat" cream cheese
1 (12-ounce) container "free" whipped topping
1 (8-ounce) container "free" whipped topping
2 chocolate cookie pie shells or graham cracker pie shells

Mix the sugar, peanut butter, and cream cheese with an electric mixer until fluffy.
Fold in the 12-ounce container of whipped topping. Pour into the pie crusts.
Use the 8-ounce cool whip to "frost" the top of the pie. Keep refrigerated.

Janice Roger's Favorite Pecan Pie

This pecan pie is unique because the syrup is cooked before the pie is put in the oven. YUM!

½ cup sugar
1 cup light corn syrup
¼ cup unsalted butter
¼ teaspoon salt
3 eggs, beaten
½ teaspoon vanilla
1 cup pecans, toasted
1 unbaked 9-inch pie shell

Combine sugar, corn syrup, butter and salt in a small saucepan. Bring just to a boil. Pour the syrup slowly over the beaten eggs stirring constantly. Cool. Add the pecans, and vanilla.
Pour the mixture into the pie crust. Bake in a preheated 400 oven for 10 minutes. Reduce oven temperature to 375° and bake 35-40 minutes longer.

Southern Pecan Pie

This is the recipe of my late cousin Joyce Howard Carter. Joyce was the past President of the Garden Clubs of Florida, and was a resident of Chipley, Florida for many years. Her brother Sonny was kind enough to share her cherished recipe. The recipe is really the same as the one above, but Joyce used Crisco instead of butter. Delicious!

½ cup sugar
¼ cup Crisco
1-1/2 cups dark Karo syrup
½ teaspoon salt
3 eggs, beaten
½ teaspoon vanilla
1 cup chopped pecans
1 prepared 9-inch pie crust

Combine the sugar, Crisco, Karo and salt and bring to a boil. Slowly pour hot mixture into beaten eggs, stirring constantly to keep eggs from cooking. Cool. Add vanilla and pecans to the cooled mixture. Pour into a prepared pie crust and bake at 400° for 10 minutes and turn down to 350° for 35 minutes or until the pie is set and a knife comes out clean when inserted in the center. Cool before cutting.

John's Island Sweet Potato Pie

My son Ed and I both love this pie!

1 deep dish (9-inch) pie crust of your choice

Praline Mixture:
3 tablespoons softened butter
1/3 cup firmly packed dark brown sugar
1/3 cup chopped pecans, toasted

Place the pie crust in the pie plate. Mix the butter, brown sugar, and chopped pecans.
Press the mixture lightly into the pie crust with your fingers. Bake in a preheated *425° oven for 5 minutes. Cool. Prepare the pie filling.
Note: You can toast pecans in the microwave by placing the chopped pecans on a plate and micro-waving on high for 1-2 minutes, depending on the power of your microwave.
*Reduce the oven temperature to 350° for the pie.

Sweet potato mixture:
3 large eggs, lightly beaten
1 cup evaporated milk
1-1/2 cup baked, mashed sweet potato
½ cup sugar
½ cup firmly packed brown sugar
1 teaspoon salt
1 teaspoon cinnamon
¼ teaspoon ground cloves
¼ teaspoon freshly grated nutmeg

Combine the ingredients in a large mixing bowl and beat at medium speed, or if you want a more solid pie, mix with a fork. Pour this mixture over the cooled praline mixture in the pie shell. Don't over fill. Bake in a *350° oven for about 50 minutes or until the pie is set. Cool before cutting. Serve with cinnamon whipped cream.

Cinnamon Whipped Cream

1 cup heavy cream
¼ cup sugar
½ teaspoon cinnamon and more to sprinkle on top

Whip the heavy cream, gradually adding the sugar, until soft peaks form. Fold in the cinnamon. Use a dollop for each pie serving. Sprinkle lightly with cinnamon.

Desserts

Berry Summer Pudding w/Grand Marnier Whipped Cream

While I was attending Le Cordon Bleu in Ottawa, I lived in a bed and breakfast. Every evening after school I would walk down to the market at Rideau and try to decide where I would have dinner among the many excellent restaurants to choose from. One in particular stood out this late summer evening. It was in an old brick building and the white tablecloths and silver was just what I needed after being away from home, and feeling it! One of my favorite desserts served there was an English Berry Summer Pudding.

Pudding:
1-12oz. Package frozen mixed berries
3 cups sliced strawberries
½ cup blueberries
1/3 cup water
1-2/3 cups sugar
3 tablespoons Grand Marnier
1(16 ounce) loaf Challah

Grand Marnier Whipped Cream:
1 cup heavy cream
¼ cup sugar
2 tablespoons Grand Marnier
1 teaspoon vanilla

Cook berries in sugar and water for 5 minutes. While berries are cooking remove crust from bread. When the berry mixture has cooked, add the Grand Marnier to the berry mixture. With a ladle, spoon a small amount of the berry mixture into the bottom of a soufflé, casserole dish or Charlotte mold. Place a layer of bread on top of the berry mixture. Using the soup ladle, spoon another layer of berries over the bread. Keep layering the bread and berries until the berries and juice are gone. Place a piece of waxed paper or plastic wrap over the top of the mixture and weigh it down with a saucer and weight on top of the saucer, such as a can and place the mixture in the refrigerator.

When ready to serve, unmold on a cake pedestal. Place a strawberry fan on top and sprinkle blueberries around the plate. Slice with a sharp knife.

To make the whipped cream: Place the cold cream in a clean mixing bowl and whip until frothy. Add the sugar, vanilla and Grand Marnier and continue whipping until soft peaks form. Keep refrigerated until ready to use. Serve a dollop of whipped cream on the pudding slice.

Berry Sabayon

I went to my mother's for Sunday luncheon. She served grilled chicken salad (recipe in the salad section) with fresh fruit.

Berry Sabayon was our delicious dessert. Mother was diabetic so she used an artificial sweetener for this dessert. I couldn't tell the difference. It was the almond extract that made the difference in the taste.

Raspberries
Blueberries
Strawberries
Artificial sweetener
1 small package sugar—free instant vanilla pudding mix
Low-fat milk
2 heaping tablespoons low-fat sour cream
½ teaspoon almond extract (more if desired)

Wash and cut the strawberries if too big. Place fruit in a bowl. Sprinkle with your favorite artificial sweetener.

Mix the sugar free pudding according to package direction, using low fat milk. Add the sour cream and almond extract.

Place berries in goblets. Pour some of the pudding mix over the top. Serve.

Lakeside Inn Banana Torte

Crust:
2 (11-ounce) boxes vanilla wafers
2 sticks butter, melted
¼ cup sugar

Filling:
2 sticks butter, melted
24 ounces confectioner's sugar

Topping:
1 (24-ounce) bottle chocolate syrup
1 (20-ounce) can crushed pineapple, drained
6-8 bananas
Lemon juice
2 cups whipping cream, whipped or 4 cups" Cool Whip Free"
½ cup maraschino cherries
1 cup chopped walnuts, or pecans, toasted

Crust: Crush vanilla wafers and mix in 1 cup of the melted butter and the granulated sugar. Spray a 9 x 13 x 2-inch glass dish. Spread the wafer mixture on the bottom to form a crust.
Filling: Mix the remaining 1 cup of melted butter and the powdered sugar until creamy and pour or spread evenly over the crust.
Topping: Top with the chocolate syrup to form the next layer. Drain the pineapple and spread over the chocolate layer. Slice the bananas; dip lightly in lemon juice to keep from discoloring. Place a layer of bananas on top of the pineapple layer. Cover with whipped cream and garnish with cherries and nuts. Place the torte in the freezer for 24 hours. Prior to serving, place in the refrigerator to thaw enough to slice. Serves 12.

Springtime Blueberry Cream Cheese Dessert

Another great recipe from Janice Rogers.

Crust:
1 cup flour
1 cup chopped nuts
1 stick butter

Mix all ingredients and press into the bottom of a 13 x 9-inch glass baking dish.
Cook for 20 minutes at 350°. Cool.

Filling:
1 (8-ounce) package cream cheese
1-1/4 cups confectioners' sugar
1 can blueberry pie filling

Mix the confectioners sugar, and cream cheese and spread on the cooled crust. Spread a can of blueberry pie filling on top. Cover with sweetened whipped cream or whipped topping, sprinkle with toasted pecans and refrigerate until ready to serve.

Sweetened whipped topping:
2 cups heavy cream
¼ cup sugar

Place cream in a mixer with whisk attachment. Whip until it has started to thicken. Gradually add the sugar. Stop the mixer when light peaks form. Otherwise you will have whipped butter. Spread over the blueberry mixture.

Pumpkin Cheesecake

4 (8-ounce) packages cream cheese
1-1/2 cups packed dark brown sugar
¼ cup all-purpose flour
1 teaspoon cinnamon
1 teaspoon allspice
¼ teaspoon ground ginger
½ teaspoon vanilla
Pinch of salt
5 eggs
1 (16-ounce) can solid pack pumpkin

With an electric mixer, mix cream cheese, packed brown sugar, flour, spices and pumpkin and mix until smooth, scraping down the sides of the bowl once or twice while mixing. While the mixer is still turned off, add 2 whole eggs. Blend at medium speed until eggs are mixed into the cream cheese mixture. Add 3 more whole eggs and mix until the eggs are blended in, scraping down the sides of the bowl. Pour the mixture into a buttered and floured (9-inch) spring form pan. Bake in a preheated 250° oven for 2-1/2 hours.

Kahlúa Cheesecake

Cheesecake:
4 (8-ounce) containers cream cheese
1-1/4 cups white sugar
¼ cup dark brown sugar, firmly packed
¼ cup flour
½ teaspoon rich instant coffee or espresso powder
3 tablespoons Kahlúa
5 eggs

Topping:
1 small package chocolate chips
½ teaspoon instant coffee or espresso powder
3 tablespoons Kahlúa

In a large mixing bowl with a paddle beater, place cream cheese, brown and white sugars, flour, instant coffee and Kahlúa. Mix until all ingredients are mixed well and cream cheese is smooth. Add the eggs one at a time, beating well to blend. Set aside. Melt chocolate chips over hot water, or in the microwave until melted. Add coffee and Kahlúa and 2 cups of the cream cheese mixture to the melted chocolate chips. Pour the plain cream cheese mixture into a buttered 9-inch spring form pan. Add the chocolate-cream cheese mixture to the top and swirl. Smooth the surface. Bake in a preheated 250° oven for 1 hour and 45 minutes. Let cool slightly with the oven door open. Refrigerate until chilled. Remove spring form pan. 10 servings.

Chocolate Pots de Crème

Custard:
3 cups heavy cream
4 ounces good quality semi-sweet chocolate, chopped
1 teaspoon brandy (also use your favorite liqueur or vanilla)
7 egg yolks
½ cup sugar

Preheat the oven to 350°. Combine the cream, chopped chocolate and liqueur in the top of a double boiler and heat, stirring, until chocolate has melted and the ingredients are well blended.
In a medium bowl, combine the egg yolks and sugar, just blending until combined with a wire whisk. Pour a little of the hot cream mixture into the yolks, whisking as you go so that you don't scramble the eggs. Gradually add the remaining cream mixture to the yolk mixture and combine well. Strain into eight 4-ounce ramekins. Bake the custards in a hot water bath one-third up the sides of the ramekins. Lay a buttered sheet of wax paper on top of the ramekins. Bake for 20-25 minutes until still slightly jiggly in the center. Cool before serving or refrigerate and served chilled.
Note: I put a tea kettle on and put hot water in the baking pan to make a hot water bath.

To top this delicious recipe off, I'd like to share the little extra special touch that I make for the topping.

Whipped Cream Topping:
1 cup heavy cream
¼ cup sugar
1 teaspoon vanilla
½ cup hazelnuts, toasted

Whip the cream, adding sugar gradually. Add vanilla. Whip until the peaks are soft. Add to the top of the chilled Pots de Crème. Sprinkle with hazelnuts.

Chocolate Soufflé

Chef Eric Crane was the Executive Pastry Chef at The Greenbrier when I was there. He gave our class hand-typed recipes to use, such as the chocolate soufflé and the cold lime soufflé, the vanilla sauce and sabayon sauce. These recipes were not in The Greenbrier Cookbook, so I am lucky to have them.

2 cups milk
1 teaspoon vanilla extract
½ cup butter, softened
½ cup flour
4 tablespoons semi sweet chocolate, melted
5 egg yolks
5 egg whites
2/3 cup sugar

Bring milk and vanilla to a boil. Pre-mix butter and flour, then add to the boiling milk. Cook until stiff. Put the mixture into a mixing bowl and mix at medium speed to cool. After mixture has cooled some, add egg yolks. Then add the melted chocolate.
Beat the egg whites and sugar to a meringue and fold into the base mixture.
Pour mixture into a buttered and sugared dish to within ½-inch of the top. Bake at 350° for approximately 30-40 minutes. To prevent burning, place the soufflé dish in a pan of hot water while baking. Serves 6-8.
Serve with a sabayon or vanilla sauce.

Vanilla Sauce

2 cups heavy cream
½ cup sugar
4 egg yolks
1 tablespoon flour
1 tablespoon vanilla extract
¼ teaspoon salt
2 scoops vanilla ice cream

Combine cream and sugar in a two quart sauce pan and bring just to a boil. Remove from heat. Beat egg yolks, flour, vanilla extract and salt and stir in a little of the hot cream. Add this mixture to the rest of the hot cream. Cook stirring constantly (do not overcook) until just thickened. Remove from the heat and add ice cream, stirring until melted. Strain. Serve hot or cold. Makes 1 quart.

Sabayon Sauce

4 egg yolks
½ cup white wine
¾ cup sugar
4 tablespoons Grand Marnier

Beat all ingredients in a stainless steel bowl over hot water bath. This will come up 3-4 times the original volume. Great served on the Chocolate Soufflé. Serves 4-8. Or one if you are the cook and you get there first.

Kahlúa Mousse (Frozen Whipped Topping)

2 cups frozen whipped topping, thawed
½ cup heavy cream
2 tablespoons unsweetened cocoa powder
1 tablespoons instant coffee
3 tablespoons granulated sugar
6 tablespoons Kahlúa
Extra whipped topping
Chocolate Sprinkles

In a medium bowl, whip the Cool Whip with the ½ cup heavy cream until stiff peaks form. Gently stir in the cocoa powder, instant coffee, and sugar. Mix well. Add the Kahlúa and stir thoroughly. Spoon into 6 dessert dishes or wine goblets and place in the refrigerator. Chill. Sprinkle the top with a dollop of whipped cream and chocolate sprinkles. Serves 6.

Kahlúa Mousse (whipped Cream)

1-1/2 cups heavy cream
2 tablespoon unsweetened cocoa powder
1 tablespoon. instant coffee
3 tablespoons sugar
6 tablespoons Kahlúa
Extra whipped cream for topping
Shaved Chocolate

Whip cream until peaks form. Stir in cocoa powder, instant coffee and sugar. Mix well. Add Kahlúa and mix well. Spoon into 6 dessert dishes and place in the refrigerator. When ready to serve, top with a spoon of whipped cream and sprinkle on chocolate shavings.

Cold Lime Soufflé

¾ cup fresh lime juice
½ ounce gelatin (1 tablespoon)
1 cup sugar
6 egg yolks
3 tablespoons lime zest
1 cup heavy cream
6 egg yolks
½ cup sugar

Heat lime juice and gelatin together in a double boiler over simmering water. In a bowl, beat the yolks, sugar, and lime zest over simmering water and continue beating until mixture is creamy and thick. Add the heated gelatin and lime mixture to the yolk mixture. Allow to cool.
Whip the cream then fold into the cooled lime mixture. Whip the egg whites and sugar to make a meringue and fold the meringue into the lime mixture. Prepare 8 small soufflé cups with collars and pour into cups. Refrigerate. Decorate with whipped cream and lime zest. You can also make a large soufflé with this recipe. Makes 8 small soufflé cups.

Crème Brulée

I love the crème Brulée served at The Greenbrier so I asked Rikki Senn, the cooking school director for the recipe. A smiling Rikki brought me the recipe before I left to go home. I know you will enjoy this recipe for Crème Brulée as much as I have over the years.

8 egg yolks
1-1/2 cups sugar
2 cups heavy cream
½ vanilla bean or 1 teaspoon vanilla extract

Mix the yolks and sugar together. Heat the cream with the vanilla bean to a boiling point. Remove from the heat and stir gradually into the egg mixture. If using the vanilla bean, remove at this point. Pour the custard into individual custard dishes. Bake in a hot water bath at 350° for 25-30 minutes or until set. Cool and top with sugar or brown sugar and place under the broiler until the sugar caramelizes.
Serve cold. Serves 5-6.

Huguenot Torte

I have heard my mother say a hundred times that this is her favorite dessert. It remained her favorite dessert until her death in 2005.

4 eggs
3 cups sugar
8 tablespoons flour
5 teaspoons baking soda
½ teaspoon salt
2 cups chopped tart cooking apples
2 cups chopped pecans (toasted)
2 teaspoons vanilla

Beat whole eggs with an electric mixer until very frothy and light lemon colored. Add the other ingredients in the order given. Pour into 2 well buttered baking pans about 8 x 12-inches. Bake in a preheated 325° oven for about 40-45 minutes until crusty and brown. To serve, remove with a spatula. Top with whipped cream and more chopped toasted pecans. Or make 16 individual servings.

Poached Pears with Dark Chocolate Sauce

8 large pears such as red D'anjou, or Bosc
1-1/2 cups sugar
1 quart water
6 to 9 cloves
2 teaspoons lemon peel
1 cinnamon stick
(2 tablespoons orange zest—optional)

1 jar Smucker's "Dove" Dark Chocolate Sauce
Warmed slightly in the microwave

In a saucepan or Dutch oven large enough to hold the pears, bring sugar, water, cloves, lemon peel, and cinnamon stick to a boil. Boil for 10 minutes. While the sugar mixture is boiling, peel the pears. Place the pears in the cooking sugar mixture and reduce the heat to a simmer. Cover, and poach until pears are very tender. That would be when you have no resistance from a knife or fork inserted into the thickest part of the pears. When pears are done, remove them from the liquid and set aside to cool. Cool the liquid. Place the pears in a container and pour the pear liquid over them. Keep refrigerated until ready to serve.

When ready to serve, warm the dark chocolate sauce in the microwave until it is pourable. Place the pears on serving dishes and pour or spoon the chocolate sauce over them. About two tablespoons for each pear will be enough. Serves 8.

Lemon Curd

1 stick unsalted butter
1-1/4 cups sugar
Grated zest and juice of 2 large lemons
3 eggs beaten

Put the butter, sugar, lemon juice and zest into a double boiler or into a heat-proof bowl over barely simmering water. Stir the mixture with a wooden spoon until the sugar has dissolved.
Remove the pan from the heat and stir a few spoonfuls into the beaten eggs. Then stir the eggs into the lemon mixture. Replace the mixture over the heat until the mixture thickens and coats the back of a spoon. Strain to remove any "scrambles egg." Let mixture cool before placing on a cake or ice cream. Refrigerate any unused portion.
Serve on scones with clotted cream or put this between Victoria cake layers.

Apple Dumplings

2 Gala apples, peeled and quartered
1 can crescent rolls
1 cup sugar
1 cup water
1 stick butter
Cinnamon

Stretch the dough to make it thinner. Wrap the apples in dough. Cover the top of the apple tops well, but don't worry too much about the bottom.
Boil the sugar, water and butter enough to dissolve the sugar.
Pour this mixture over the apples. Sprinkle with cinnamon. Bake in a preheated 350° oven about 30 minutes or until golden brown. Cool for 15 minutes before serving.

Sandra's Peach Cobbler

My cousin Sandra Dodd shared this recipe with me. It was her father's recipe for cobbler. The day after mother died, we got together in my mother's kitchen and cooked. It was in the summer, and we decided that we would spend our time that day making a good old-fashioned picnic type dinner. This is one of the dishes that we made. Nothing soothes a hurting heart like good food.

½ stick butter
1 cup self-rising flour
¾ cup sugar
¾ cup buttermilk
3-4 cups sliced peaches

Melt the butter and pour it into an 8 x 8 inch oven-proof dish. Mix all ingredients except the fruit and pour it over the melted butter. Place peaches on top. Do not stir. Bake in a pre-heated 350° oven until crusty and golden brown.

*I put a couple of tablespoons sugar over the fruit. To find out if the cobbler batter has cooked, use the tip of a sharp knife in the center of the cobbler. If it comes out with batter on it, let it cook a little longer.

English Sticky Pudding with Caramel Sauce

I picked up this recipe in England a few years ago. It fits right into our southern palate with the caramel sauce. Who could not love it! I have to admit that I have not tested this recipe, or I would have eaten it all!

Pudding:
1 cup water
¾ cup chopped pitted dates
1 teaspoon baking soda
½ stick butter, softened
1 cup sugar
1 cup all-purpose flour
2 eggs
½ teaspoon vanilla extract

Caramel Sauce:
1 cup dark brown sugar
1 cup clotted cream or heavy cream (unwhipped)
1 stick plus 1 tablespoon butter
½ teaspoon vanilla extract
Cream for serving

Pudding: Stir in a saucepan the 1 cup water, dates and baking soda. Cook over medium heat to soften the dates. Cool slightly. In a mixing bowl, add 1 cup flour, 1 cup sugar, and the softened butter. Add an egg to the flour mixture and blend well. Add the second egg. Now stir the cooled dates into the flour mixture, and add the vanilla. Bake in an 8 x 11 inch baking dish that has been lined with parchment paper at 325° for about 40 minutes. When done, cool the pudding on a rack.
Caramel Sauce: Melt butter in a saucepan. Add the brown sugar. Stir until combined. Add the vanilla. Blend in the cream and boil for 3 minutes. The texture should coat the back of a spoon. Serve over the pudding with a touch of extra clotted cream, or whipping cream on top. Serves 6.

Strawberry Amaretto Romanoff

This is another delicious recipe that mother gave me.

4 cups fresh strawberries, halved if small, quartered if large
½ cup Amaretto or your favorite almond liqueur
½ cup sugar

1 cup heavy whipping cream
2 tablespoons sugar
1 teaspoon almond extract
Toasted almond slices

Stir together the strawberries, Amaretto and sugar. Chill for 3-4 hours or overnight. Spoon into Champagne bowls or flutes.
Beat heavy cream, sugar and almond extract until lightly whipped. Top the berries with a spoon of the cream. Top the cream with sliced almonds

Fat Free Strawberry Ice Cream

3 cups fat free half and half
1 (14-ounce) can fat free sweetened condensed milk
1 cup pureed strawberries
1 tablespoon vanilla extract
Red food coloring

Mix all ingredients and pour into an ice cream freezer container. Freeze according to manufacturers directions.

Vanilla Custard Ice Cream

When I was a child we would go to my grandparent's home on Sunday afternoon and make real home-made ice cream. My mother made and brought the cooked custard and the ice cream freezer was set up on the back porch near the well where it was cool. We cranked the ice cream until it was so cold and creamy, and I could hardly wait to get a giant bowl of that luscious ice cream. We had to eat fast or it would melt in the heat of a southern summer.

¼ cup all-purpose flour
¼ teaspoon salt
1 quart milk
1 quart half and half
1-1/2 cups sugar
4 large eggs, lightly beaten
1 tablespoon vanilla

Combine the sugar, flour, and salt in a large heavy Dutch oven. Gradually add the milk, stirring until smooth. Cook mixture over medium heat, stirring constantly, until thickened about 10 minutes. Gradually stir in one fourth of the hot mixture into the beaten eggs. Add back to the remaining hot mixture, stirring constantly.

Continue to cook over medium heat, stirring constantly until the mixture reaches 160 degrees. Remove from heat and stir in the half and half and vanilla. Chill.

Pour the mixture into a 1-gallon hand-turned or electric ice cream freezer. Freeze according to manufacturers directions. Pack freezer with additional ice and salt. Let Stand for 1 hour before serving. Make 2-1/2 quarts.

Christmas Memories

My sister Margaret and I peeped into the living room. Sitting on the sofa watching the trains go around under the Christmas tree was our grandfather. Our name for mother's father was "Poppy" and Poppy was visiting us from Mobile so he could hunt in the country during the holidays.

We always enjoyed being with Poppy because he told us lots of stories. But, early this morning we just wanted to know if he had seen Santa. Poppy told us that he had not. Well, we were up! We were going to stay up! No daylight yet. How could we know if our swing set that we had asked Santa for was in the yard? Santa came through on the trains, though. Yippee!

Christmas memories! How great they are! Early that morning Sarah would come and make breakfast for us. Later in the day we would have a feast of all the traditional food that my mother and father had in their families when they were growing up. A combination of traditions would happen again when I married. And, so my sons will have with their families.

Today, we still have most of the same food that we had years ago. We might have added a few things here and there. My son Rob now makes a "beer butt turkey" on his grill and son Ed has expanded his menu since he travels all over the world now and eats things that I wouldn't. Good for him, though.

One item that has stayed on our menu is my mother's Ambrosia. Said to be "food for the gods" it has been served at our Christmas table for as long as I can remember. And, my mother said that it has been served at her table and her mother's table as long as both could remember. My mother won't be with us this year, but her Ambrosia will continue to grace our Southern table as long as a coconut and an orange are growing on this earth! Happy Holidays!

My Mother's Ambrosia

Freshly grated coconut (must be fresh)
Orange sections
Pineapple chunks from a fresh pineapple
Maraschino Cherries

Put equal amounts of each item except the cherries in a large bowl. Sweeten to taste. Transfer to a crystal bowl or if you have a big crowd, to a large punch bowl. Put cherries on top for decoration. My mother had a large crystal punch bowl that was a gift from her father. She always served the Ambrosia in that. It was always beautiful, and she was always so proud of her Ambrosia!

Mother's Fruit Roll

1 (12-ounce) package vanilla wafers, crushed
1 cup chopped candied pineapple
1 cup chopped candied cherries
2 cups chopped pecans, toasted
1 (14-ounce) can condensed milk
Sifted powdered sugar

Combine the first 5 ingredients, mixing well. Divide into 3 equal portions; roll each into an 11-inch log. Roll each log in the powdered sugar and wrap in plastic. Refrigerate several hours or until firm; cut into ½-inch slices, reshaping slices if necessary. 5 dozen slices.

Mother's Divinity

2-1/2 cups sugar
½ cup corn syrup
1/8 teaspoon salt
2/3 cup water
2 egg whites, stiffly beaten
1-1/2 cup chopped pecans, toasted
1 tablespoon vanilla
Pecan halves
Maraschino cherry halves, completely dry

Combine sugar, corn syrup, salt and water. Cook until a small amount forms a soft ball (234-240°) on a candy thermometer) when dropped into a cup of cold water.

Take out ½ cup of the mixture and cook the rest until it forms a hard ball (250-265°) when dropped in cold water. Pour the ½ cup of syrup slowly over the stiffly beaten egg whites, beating constantly in an electric mixer. Continue beating; add the remaining syrup. Add nuts and vanilla and keep beating until it thickens and becomes heavy. Pour into buttered pan and cut when cold or drop with a teaspoon on a buttered surface or parchment paper.

*Mother's method of checking to see if it had reached the right stage was to throw some of the mixture against the refrigerator and see if it clicks. If it did, then it was ready. Mother would drop by teaspoons onto wax paper. She would put a cherry on some and pecan halves on the rest.

Proseco & Oranges

¾ cup sugar
¾ cup orange marmalade
1-3/4 cups Proseco (Italian sparkling wine)
10 large naval oranges, peeled and sectioned*
3/4 cup sliced almonds, toasted

Combine the sugar and marmalade in a small saucepan and cook until sugar dissolves. Remove from heat, and add Proseco to the marmalade mixture. Pour over oranges. Chill. Serve in Champagne bowls or tulips and top with toasted almonds. If serving a large crowd, just put the oranges in a punch bowl.
Note: To peel oranges, slice a piece off the top and the bottom. Then take a small sharp knife and cut down toward the bottom of the orange taking off the white pith with the peel. Now cut between the sections to get an orange slice without pith or membrane.

Oranges in Grand Marnier

Oh Wendy, where are you? I made your favorite!

2 cups orange sections
2 teaspoons sugar
2 tablespoons Grand Marnier

Cut the peel away from the orange. Cut the orange sections out of the membrane so that you have an orange section without membrane or pith.
Place orange sections in a bowl. Add sugar and Grand Marnier. Great for gift giving!
* See directions for Oranges in Proseco to peel an orange.

Eggnog Raspberry Trifle

3 cups eggnog
2 cups heavy cream
3 tablespoon sugar
1 teaspoon Amaretto
1 teaspoon vanilla
1 (12-ounce) jar seedless raspberry jam or preserves
3 cups raspberries
Amaretto for sprinkling
2 packages lady fingers
1-1/2 cups toasted almonds

Topping:
1 cup heavy cream
3 tablespoons sugar
1 tablespoon Amaretto

Whip 2 cups heavy cream with 3 tablespoons sugar. Fold in the eggnog, 1 teaspoon Amaretto and the vanilla.

Separate the lady fingers. Spread one side of the ladyfingers with raspberry jam. Put flat sides back together to make a sandwich. Place a layer of raspberry jam sandwiched ladyfingers in the bottom of a trifle dish. Sprinkle lightly with 1 teaspoon amaretto.

Place a layer of eggnog cream over the ladyfingers. Spread about 1 cup fresh raspberries over the top of the eggnog-cream mixture. Sprinkle with toasted almonds. Keep layering exactly the same until all the custard has been used. This will make 3 layers with the third layer being the top. Whip the remaining 1 cup of heavy cream with 3 tablespoons sugar and 1 tablespoon Amaretto. Place this over the last layer and sprinkle with toasted almonds, and the remaining 1 cup of raspberries. Place in the refrigerator for several hours or overnight. Refrigerate any leftover portion.

*Once I put too much eggnog into the cream and the cream lost its whip, so I added the rest of the eggnog and rewhipped it. It came together again just fine after about a minute of whipping.

Sherried Fruit Casserole

This is one of my friend Ellen's family traditions at Christmas.

1 medium can sliced pineapple
1 medium can peach halves
1 medium can pear halves
1 medium can apricot halves
1 jar spiced red apple rings (if not available use 1 large can Royal Anne Cherries, drained)
1 jar maraschino cherries
2 tablespoons self-rising flour or cornstarch
1/2 cup light brown sugar
1 stick butter
1 cup dry sherry

Drain fruit. Arrange in a large deep baking dish. In top of a double boiler, melt butter and add flour and blend thoroughly. Add sugar and sherry. Stir until smooth and thickened. Pour sauce over fruit. Cover and refrigerate overnight. Before serving, heat in a 350° degree oven until hot and bubbly. Serves 8-10.

Bourbon Soufflé

My mother would say "Bourbon is not just for fruitcake my dear!" This recipe from one of my Greenbrier classes will make you forget all the money you just spent!

4 cups milk
2 tablespoons gelatin
1 cup sugar
10 egg yolks (reserve whites separately)
1-1/2 cups bourbon
3 cups whipping cream
¼ cup sugar
1 cup egg whites

Heat the milk. Mix the gelatin and sugar together and add to the hot milk, stirring as you add. Place yolks in a bowl and add some of the hot milk mixture and mix well. Pour egg mixture into the milk mixture. Add bourbon and cool.

When the bourbon mixture starts setting up, whip the cream and set aside. Then whip the egg whites and sugar to make a meringue. Fold the whipped cream first, and then fold the meringue to the bourbon mixture.

Take a 2-quart soufflé bowl and put a paper collar one inch above and one inch below the soufflé top. Fill the bowl with the mixture and refrigerate. Add setting for several hours, remove the collar and decorate with more whipped cream. * For the collar, use parchment paper or waxed paper. To hold in place, tape or string will work. Makes 1 (2 quart) soufflé.

Date Nut Rolls

(Great for Gift Giving)

½ cup butter
1 cup dark brown sugar
1 (7.5-ounce) package dates

Mix all together in a pan. Cook over low heat until mixture bubbles. Simmer for 5 minutes longer. Remove from the stove and add the following ingredients except the confectioner's sugar:

1 cup chopped pecans, toasted
1 cup sweetened coconut
2 cup rice cereal (crispy)
1 teaspoon vanilla
1/8 teaspoon salt
Confectioner's sugar

Add this mixture to the cooked mixture above and roll into small ball. Then roll in confectioner's sugar.
Note: You have to work while the mixture is hot, so take care with hands. You might want to wear rubber gloves.

Peanut Butter Cup Cookies

Great for gift giving! My friend John Matula in Chicago used this recipe for a cookie swap.

1 roll refrigerated peanut butter cookie dough
2 packages miniature peanut butter cups

Lightly spray a mini muffin tin with non-stick cooking spray.
Preheat oven to 350°. Cut dough into ¾ inch slices and the slices into quarters. Place the quarter pieces into the mini-muffin tin.
Bake for 8 minutes. As soon as you remove the tin from the oven, put an unwrapped peanut butter cup in the center. Let cool slightly before removing from muffin tin.

Brandied Cranberry Cake

This Cake is delicious! I promise. It is also a great holiday gift cake. Wrap it in cellophane, tie a red ribbon around it, and deliver it to the luckiest recipient ever. Happy Holidays!

3 cups all-purpose flour
2-1/3 cups sugar
1 teaspoon baking powder
½ teaspoon soda
1 teaspoon salt
4 eggs
4 ounces cream cheese, room temperature
1 stick soft butter
1 teaspoon vanilla extract
1 teaspoon orange extract
1 cup buttermilk
2 cups brandied cranberries (see recipe below)

Preheat oven to 325°. Spray a 12 cup tube or bundt pan with a floured baking spray. Mix flour, sugar, soda, baking powder, salt, eggs, cream cheese, butter, buttermilk, and extracts in a mixer bowl. Beat on medium speed for 3 minutes. Remove from the mixer and fold in the brandied cranberries. Bake for 1 hour and 10 minutes or until a cake tester comes out clean.

Brandied Cranberries

3 (12- ounce) bags fresh or frozen cranberries
3 cups sugar
½ cup brandy

Place cranberries in a single layer on a two foil lined 15 x 10 x 1-inch jelly roll pan. Pour sugar over the cranberries. Cover tightly with foil. Bake at 350° for 1 hour. Spoon the cranberries into a large bowl. Gently stir in brandy. Refrigerate until ready to use. Makes 2-1/2 cups.

Mommy's Graham Cracker Cake

Mommy, my mother's mother, made this every Christmas. Thanks to my cousin Sandra, for giving it to me from her collection of our grandmother's recipes.

Cake:
1 box graham crackers, crushed
2 sticks butter
2 cups sugar
5 eggs, beaten
1 cup grated coconut (I use Baker's Angel flake)
1 cup chopped pecans, toasted
2 teaspoons baking powder
1 teaspoon vanilla

Frosting:
1 small can crushed pineapple, undrained
2 cups heavy cream, whipped with 3 T. sugar and 1 teaspoon vanilla

For the cake: Mix all ingredients together. Do not beat with an electric mixer. Pour into a tube pan. Bake for 1-1/2 hours at 300° beginning with a cold oven—in other words—Do Not preheat the oven. Let cake cool for 20 minutes before removing from the pan. Cool before frosting.
For the frosting: After cake cools, spread pineapple over cake. Spread whipped cream mixed with the sugar and vanilla over the pineapple.

Mama Irene's Mincemeat Fruitcake

I didn't have a lot of my Grandmother Irene's precious recipes until my Aunt Elizabeth Henderson (Aunt Sis) in Hattiesburg sent me several of them. I'll never be able to thank her for doing such a sweet thing for me. This fruitcake is one that I remember as a child. It's great during the holidays with a cup of tea.

2-1/2 cups flour
1-1/2 teaspoons baking powder
½ teaspoon soda
½ teaspoon salt
1 (1-pound) jar mincemeat
1 cup raisins
1 cup chopped pecans
1 cup sugar
1 stick butter, melted
1 teaspoon vanilla
2 eggs

Combine the first 4 ingredients, sift and set aside. Then mix the mincemeat, raisins, nuts, sugar, melted butter and vanilla. Add eggs, one at a time, beating well with each addition. Fold in dry ingredients which have been sifted together. Pour into a lightly greased tube cake pan, lining the bottom with waxed paper. Bake in a slow 325° oven for 1 to 1-1/2 hours. Remove from pan at once when done.

Mama Irene's Lane Cake

My friends know that I like cooking magazines and one of them recently gave me a copy of Saveur. To my delightful surprise it contained a recipe for Lane Cake. Edna Lewis and Scott Peacock had resurrected this Southern beauty to share with a new generation who love to cook. This prompted me to search through my box of newspaper clippings and old recipes to find my grandmother's recipe for Lane Cake.

For those of you who have never had the pleasure of having this delectable dessert, it's a white cake, with a cooked filling of coconut, raisins, and pecans. For those of you who have had Lane Cake, I know that you are thinking of your grandmother right now, too.

My grandmother lived in a Victorian farmhouse. It was built before the turn of the century, sat high off the ground and overlooked the town. It was a large old house. Grandmother had decided long ago that the dining room table and sideboard would be in the long hall that went through the center of the house. It was cool in winter and summer, and would seat the entire family when we all gathered for the holidays. In the winter, the long table was the perfect place for her wonderful cakes. And, especially, the grandest lady of them all, the Lane Cake.

Unlike Mrs. Emma Rylander Lane's original Lane Cake recipe, my grandmother embellished her cake. Instead of following the recipe and just putting the filling between the layers, she also covered the entire cake with filling, and then iced the cake with seven-minute frosting. It was glorious on a tall pedestal cake stand. It was Christmas! It was Southern!

I know that every family has developed its own tradition over the years, but I also believe that Lane Cake is one of the most Southern desserts during the holidays. Unfortunately, I have made Lane Cake only once for my family, and I have not seen it on another table or sideboard since before my grandmother's death in the 1970's.

Food has always been a part of our heritage in the South. Whether it's talking about food, or writing about food, we have memories attached. It's really important to keep those memories alive. So this year, if I can get my family together for the holidays, I am going to make a Lane Cake. I think that I would like to share my childhood tradition with them, and I have a feeling that the tradition will be enjoyed more than the cake.

I hope that during the holidays you will also share one of your childhood traditions with your family. Because when I think about it now, I realize that it took my grandmother hours to make that cake. And, I know that it was really her love that she was sharing with us.
This is my grandmother's Lane Cake recipe if you would like to share it with your family.

Mama Irene's Lane Cake

(Exactly as written)

Cake:
2 cups sugar
½ lb butter
1-1/3 cups sweet milk
3 teaspoon baking powder
3-1/2 cups cake flour
7 egg whites, stiffly beaten
1 teaspoon flavoring (vanilla-or some people used bourbon)

Cream butter and sugar until fluffy. Sift all dry ingredients. Add dry ingredients to butter mixture alternating with the milk. Add flavoring and beaten egg whites last. (There is not a temp or time or pan size. So, preheat oven to 325°. Grease and flour 3 (8 inch) cake pans. Line bottoms of pans with buttered or greased parchment paper. Bake for approximately 20 minutes and check to see if cakes are cooked by putting a toothpick or cake tester in the center of the cake until it comes out clean. Let cool in pans for 10 minutes and remove to wire racks to cool completely.

Filling:
1-1/2 cups sugar
7 egg yolks
½ lb butter or margarine
Cook in double boiler until thick and mixture coats the back of a spoon; now add
1 cup raisins
1 cup pecans (chopped and toasted)
1 cup crushed pineapple, drained
1 cup coconut (optional)

Cook for another minute and remove from heat. Cool only slightly.
Spread filling between layers and on top and sides of Cake.
When completely cooled, ice cake with your favorite 7 minute icing on the top and sides of cake.

Seven minute Icing

1-3/4 cup sugar
1 tablespoon corn starch
Pinch of salt
1/3 cup water
3 egg whites
1 teaspoon vanilla

Set the mixture except the vanilla, in the top of a double boiler, over simmering water. Beat for 7 minutes with an electric mixer. Beat in vanilla. Spread on sides and top of cake.

Breads, Rolls, Sweet Muffins, Scones & Tea Cakes

Orange & Currant Scones

I love these little scones. You can make them in the food processor. Once I forgot to add the butter to the processor so I used a microplane and grated the butter in, and the scones were still great!

1-1/4 cups self-rising flour
1/8 cup sugar
4 tablespoons butter
Zest from 1 orange
1 egg
2 ounces heavy cream
¼ cup currants

Place flour, butter and sugar in bowl of food processor with a steel blade, and mix until the mixture resembles cornmeal. Put egg and cream through the chute. Process until the dough forms a ball. Turn out onto a floured board and add the orange zest and currants. Knead several times. Cut with small biscuit cutters and place on parchment lined baking sheet. Bake at 375° degrees for 10-12 minutes, or until lightly browned. Serve with strawberry jam and Clotted cream (see index).

Mock Devonshire Cream

½ cup heavy cream
½ cup sour cream
¼ cup firmly packed brown sugar
3 teaspoons Amaretto or ¼ teaspoon almond extract or ¼ teaspoon vanilla extract

Whip heavy cream until soft peaks form. Fold into the sour cream, brown sugar, and flavoring. Refrigerate until ready to use. 4 servings.

Mock Clotted Cream

Good!

1 (8-ounce) package cream cheese, softened
1 cup heavy cream
1 cup sour cream
5 tablespoons confectioner's sugar

Combine all ingredients in a small bowl and beat with a mixer until fluffy.

Jelly Biscuits

½ cup all-purpose flour
2 teaspoon sugar
¾ teaspoon baking powder
1/8 teaspoon salt
2 tablespoon shortening
3 tablespoons milk
Milk for glaze
2-1/2 teaspoons desired flavor jelly or jam

Preheat oven to 425° degrees. Place the flour, sugar, baking powder, salt and shortening in a food processor fitted with a steel blade, and process until mixture resembles coarse crumbs. Add 3 tablespoons milk through the chute and process to form a soft dough, being careful not to over beat.
On a floured surface, knead the dough lightly 3-4 times. Roll the dough with a rolling pin to about 1/8-inch thickness.
With a 1-1/2 inch round or scalloped round cutter, cut out dough. With a ¾-inch round cutter, cut a hole in the center of half of the dough rounds. Re-roll scraps and centers as needed. Brush whole rounds lightly with additional milk.
Place the rounds with holes on top of the whole rounds. Place each stacked round 1 inch apart on an ungreased baking sheet. Spoon ¼ teaspoon desired flavor of jelly, jam or lemon curd in the center of each stacked round.
Bake in the preheated oven about 8 minutes or until golden. Remove and cool on wire racks. Approximately 10 biscuits.

Mother's Cornmeal Turnip Dumplings

My mother made the best cornmeal turnip dumplings. My husband loves the dumplings, but he won't eat the greens! This is her recipe. Use your favorite turnip green recipe for the greens.

4 heaping tablespoons self-rising cornmeal
1 heaping tablespoon flour
4 finely chopped green onions (including tender tops)
1/8 teaspoon salt and pepper
Turnip broth to moisten

Mix the meal, flour, salt and pepper, and chopped green onions. Add just enough turnip broth to moisten. Make small dumplings and place in a slowly boiling pot of turnips. Cover and cook until dumplings are done, about 20 minutes.

Richard's Best Cornbread

(Double for a larger pan of cornbread)

1/3 cup flour
1/3 cup self-rising corn meal
1 tablespoon oil plus 1 tablespoon for the pan
1 egg
½ cup buttermilk

Mix the flour and cornmeal together. Add the oil, egg and buttermilk. Heat a 6-inch skillet on the stove top with 1 tablespoon oil. When hot, add the cornbread mixture. Place the mixture in a 350° preheated oven and cook the cornbread until it is brown on top. It will be moist.

Southern Spoonbread

1-1/2 cups boiling water
1 cup cornmeal (white preferably)
1 teaspoon salt
2 tablespoons butter, melted
1 cup milk
2 large eggs, lightly beaten
2 teaspoons baking powder

Pour the water over the cornmeal, gradually stirring until smooth. Add salt and butter, stirring until blended. Cool for 10 minutes. Gradually stir in the milk and eggs. Add baking powder, stirring until blended. Pour mixture into a lightly greased 1-1/2 quart baking or soufflé dish.
Bake at 375° for 40 minutes or until lightly browned. 4-6 servings.

Janice Rogers Best Dinner Rolls

I remember the first time I had these rolls. That is how good they were! It was on my birthday and it was also Thanksgiving Day. Out of the kitchen to the table came these large yeast rolls. You could smell the yeast. Oh so good!

1 package yeast
½ cup warm water (105-115 degrees)
½ cup sugar
½ cup shortening
1-1/2 tablespoons salt
1 large egg
2 cups warm water (or milk for a richer roll)
6 cups all-purpose flour such as White Lily

Dissolve yeast in ½ cup warm water (105-115°) with a pinch of the sugar. Let yeast develop for a few minutes until bubbly.
Cream the ½ cup sugar with the ½ cup shortening and the salt. Add the egg, 2 cups of warm water and the yeast mixture together. Add 4 cups of the flour and mix well. Add enough of the remaining flour to make good soft dough. Mix well. Put the roll dough in a greased bowl, and place in the refrigerator to rise double the size. Punch down the dough. Turn out onto a lightly floured dish towel, and roll out. Pinch off enough dough to make a small ball. Place the balls on a greased baking sheet. Brush with butter. Let rise until double in size. Bake at 375° until rolls are lightly brown and done, about 20 minutes.

Good Little Rolls

2 cup buttermilk baking mix
1 stick unsalted butter, melted
1 cup light sour cream

Mix all ingredients and place them in either regular or mini muffin tins. Bake in a pre-heated 375° oven until light brown on top.

Yummy Biscuits!

1 tablespoons butter, melted
2 cups biscuit baking mix
2/3 cup buttermilk
2 teaspoons sugar
¼ teaspoon salt

Preheat the oven to 450°. In a bowl, mix the butter, biscuit mix, sugar, salt and buttermilk until well-blended. Turn the dough out onto a lightly floured surface and knead until dough is like elastic. Roll the dough out to ¾-inch and cut with a 3-inch biscuit cutter. Place on an ungreased baking sheet and bake for 10-12 minutes. Brush biscuits with butter while still hot. Makes about 8 biscuits.
*If you put the biscuits close together on the baking sheet, they will be softer.

Southern Flour Biscuits

I got this recipe at a flour seminar. I tried the biscuits and they are wonderful. It's definitely not my biscuit recipe because I couldn't make them this good!

1-1/2 cups self-rising soft southern wheat flour
1 tablespoon sugar
¼ teaspoon salt
3 tablespoons butter-flavored shortening
½ cup heavy cream
¾ cup buttermilk or sour cream
1 cup soft southern wheat flour for dipping
2 tablespoons melted butter

Preheat the oven to 450°. Spray a pan with cooking spray to keep the biscuits from sticking. Mix the flour, sugar, and salt in a bowl. With the tips of your fingers, mix the shortening into the flour until it is the consistency of meal. Stir in the cream and then the buttermilk. The dough will be slightly lumpy.
Place the 1 cup flour on a plate. With an ice-cream scoop, scoop out a biscuit size lump of dough and place it in the flour. Coat the dough, and then shake to remove excess flour, place it in the sprayed or greased baking pan. Repeat, pressing each biscuit against each other so that the biscuits are touching. Bake in the center of the oven until lightly browned. Brush the biscuits with melted butter. The recipe makes about 10 biscuits.

John's Biscuits

This is my step-father's recipe for biscuits. Really good.

1 tablespoon shortening
2 cups all-purpose soft southern wheat flour
1 tablespoon baking powder
1/8 teaspoon soda
½ teaspoon salt
1 cup + 2 tablespoons buttermilk
Vegetable oil

Mix flour, baking powder and salt. Add the shortening and blend well with a pastry blender. Add the baking soda to the buttermilk. Add the buttermilk mixture gradually to the flour mixture to make a good dough. Blend well.
Roll out the biscuits to ½ inch thickness on a floured dish towel. Cut the biscuits with a 2-inch cutter. Dip in oil and place on an oiled baking sheet. Bake in a preheated 400° oven for 8-10 minutes or until browned.

Cheese Garlic Biscuits

(Famous Restaurant Biscuits)

2 cups biscuit baking mix
2/3 cup milk
½ cup shredded Cheddar cheese
½ cup butter, melted
¼ teaspoon garlic powder

Preheat the oven to 450°. Mix baking mix, milk, and cheese until a soft dough forms. Beat vigorously for 30 seconds. Drop dough by spoonfuls onto an ungreased baking sheet. Bake 8-10 minutes until golden brown.
Mix garlic and butter. Brush garlic butter over the warm biscuits. Serve biscuits warm. 12 Biscuits.

Sesame Sandwich Rolls

Split these rolls to hold your favorite sandwich spread, ham or turkey slices.

1 tablespoon yeast
¼ cup warm water (105-115°)
2-1/3 cups all-purpose flour, divided
2 tablespoons sugar
1 teaspoon salt
¼ teaspoon baking soda
1 (8-ounce) nonfat yogurt
1 large egg
1 cup shredded reduced fat Alpine Lace cheese
Cooking spray
2 teaspoons sesame seeds, toasted

Combine yeast and warm water and a pinch of sugar in a small bowl. Let stand for 5 minutes.
Combine the yeast mixture, 1 cup of flour, sugar and next four ingredients in a large mixing bowl.
Beat the batter at low speed with an electric mixer until well blended. Beat at high speed for 2 minutes, scraping bowl down once.
Stir in remaining flour and cheese and mix well.
Divide batter between 8 mini-loaf pans. Sprinkle with toasted sesame seeds.
Cover and set in a warm place for about an hour.
Bake in a preheated 350° oven for 25 minutes or until loaves are lightly browned on top. Remove from pans to a wire rack so that steam won't form on the bottom.
*These little sandwich rolls freeze very well.

Daddy's Angel Biscuits

My daddy loves angel biscuits. Janice's cousin in Alabama makes them. This is the recipe that I use. Alabamians are famous for their Angel Biscuits.

1 package or 1 tablespoon dry yeast
2 tablespoons warm water (105-115°)
5 cups self-rising soft southern wheat flour
¼ cup sugar
½ teaspoon salt
½ teaspoon baking soda
1 cup regular or butter flavored shortening
2 cups buttermilk
Melted butter

Spray a baking sheet with baking spray. Dissolve the yeast in warm water with a pinch of the sugar from the ¼ cup. This allows the yeast to activate. Set the yeast mixture aside to become bubbly.
In a large bowl add the flour, sugar, salt and soda and mix well to blend the ingredients. Blend in the shortening until the mixture looks like coarse cornmeal. Combine the buttermilk and yeast water and add it to the flour. Stir until moistened. Turn the dough out onto a floured surface and knead several times until the dough comes together well. Roll or pat out to ½-inch thickness. Cut with a biscuit cutter the size of your choice.
A large 2-inch cutter for a meal size biscuit and a very small cutter for a cocktail biscuit. Put the biscuits close together on the baking sheet.
Cover with a warm damp cloth and let them sit for about an hour. The biscuits will not rise, but this will make them very light. Bake in a preheated 400° oven for 10-20 minutes, depending on the biscuit size or until browned. Brush with melted butter after removing from the oven.

Sweet Potato Biscuits

2-1/2 cup all-purpose flour
2 tablespoons baking powder
1 teaspoon salt
½ cup shortening
1 egg, beaten
¾ cup milk
1-1/2 cups mashed sweet potato
Melted butter

Sift the flour, baking powder, and salt into a bowl. Cut in the shortening using your fingertips, pastry blender or knives. Combine the egg, milk and sweet potatoes. Add this mixture to the flour mixture and mix well. Chill the dough.
Knead the dough lightly on a floured tea towel. Roll out to ½ inch thickness and cut with a floured biscuit cutter. Place the biscuits on a greased baking sheet. Brush the tops with melted butter. Bake at 400°for about 10 minutes.

Apple Butter Muffins

1-2/3 cups sugar
2 teaspoons baking soda
¾ teaspoons baking powder
3-1/2 cups all-purpose flour
2 teaspoons cinnamon
1(16-ounce) jar apple butter
1-1/4 cups sour cream
4 eggs lightly beaten
¾ cup vegetable oil
1 apple, red or golden delicious, finely chopped or shredded in food processor

Preheat oven to 350°. In a large bowl, combine all dry ingredients together. Stir in apple butter. In another bowl, stir together all the remaining ingredients. Add to the flour mixture, stirring well. Pour batter into paper lined muffin tins. Bake for 20 minutes or until a cake tester inserted into the center of the muffin comes out clean. 12-15 Muffins.

Double Pineapple Bread

Mother sent this recipe to me via e-mail. When she got the computer years ago, it was one of our favorite ways to send recipes back and forth to each other!

3/4 cup sugar
1/2 cup butter
2 eggs
2 (8-ounce) cans crushed pineapple, well drained
1 teaspoon vanilla
2 cups all-purpose flour
1 teaspoons baking soda
1 teaspoon baking powder
1 teaspoon ground cinnamon
1/2 teaspoon salt
1/2 teaspoon ground nutmeg
1/2 cup chopped walnuts—toasted

Beat sugar and butter until light and fluffy. Add eggs, drained pineapple and vanilla. Mix well. Combine the dry ingredients, stir in the walnuts. Pour the batter into 3 mini loaf pans (5.5 x 3) coated with cooking spray and bake at 350° for 35-40 minutes.

Chocolate Brownie Muffins

4 ounces semi-sweet chocolate, coarsely chopped
1 stick unsalted butter
1-1/2 cups all-purpose flour
¼ cup cocoa powder
2 teaspoon double acting baking powder
1 teaspoon baking soda
1/8 teaspoon salt
2 large eggs, lightly beaten
2/3 cup granulated sugar
½ cup milk
9 ounces semi-sweet chocolate chips
1 cup coarsely chopped walnuts

Preheat oven to 350°. Place the oven rack in the center of the oven. Line a muffin pan with paper or aluminum cups. In the top of a double boiler over simmering water, melt the chocolate and butter, stirring occasionally until smooth. Set the top boiler with the chocolate and butter aside and off the stove to cool.

Sift the cocoa, flour, baking powder, soda and salt into a large bowl. Whisk the dry ingredients to blend. In a medium bowl, whisk the eggs, sugar, and milk together. Add the chocolate and butter mixture to the egg mixture and whisk until blended.

With a rubber spatula, fold the chocolate-egg mixture into the flour mixture, folding only enough to blend the dry ingredients into the wet ingredients and until well moistened.

Stir in the chocolate chips and walnuts. With an ice cream scoop, fill the muffin cups ¾ full. Bake for 15-18 minutes or until springy to the touch. Cool in the pan on a wire rack. Store in an airtight container.

New England Summer Tea Bread

Another of the recipes that mother gave me in the past 10 years. I used to make this one for the farmers market. It was a good seller.

3/4 cup sugar
6 tablespoons butter, softened
4 teaspoons lemon zest
1 teaspoons lemon juice
2 cups all-purpose flour
2 eggs
1 tablespoon baking powder
¼ teaspoons salt
¾ cup milk
1 cup fresh or frozen small blueberries

Grease and flour 2 (7-1/2 x 3-1/2 x 2-inch) loaf pans. Set the loaf pans aside. In a large mixing bowl beat the sugar and butter on high until well-mixed. Beat in the eggs and lemon juice. In a small bowl, stir together the flour, baking powder, and salt. Alternately add flour mixture and milk to the butter mixture, beating until just combined. Fold in blueberries and lemon zest. Spread the batter evenly in the loaf pans. Bake in a preheated 350° oven for 40-45 minutes or until a cake tester comes out clean. Cool in the baking pans for 10 minutes, then turn out on to a wire rack to finish cooling.

Southern Apricot Tea Bread

Mother gave me this recipe the same time that she gave me the blueberry bread. It has a cream cheese center, and is good for tea time.

1 cup dried apricots cut into thin strips
½ cup golden raisins
½ stick butter at room temperature
½ cup sugar
½ cup firmly packed light brown sugar
1 egg, room temperature
2 cups all-purpose flour
2 teaspoons baking powder
½ teaspoon soda
½ teaspoons salt
3/4 cup orange juice
½ cup chopped pecans or walnuts, toasted

Cream Cheese Filling:
1/3 cup sugar
2 (3-ounce) packages cream cheese, softened
1 large egg

Preheat the oven to 350°. Combine the apricots and raisins and cover with boiling water. Allow to stand for 30 minutes. Drain. Set aside. In a separate bowl, cream together butter, sugar and brown sugar. Beat in the egg. In a separate bowl, add together the flour, baking powder, soda and salt. Add to the butter mixture alternately with the orange juice. Stir in the apricots and raisins. Pour 2/3 of the mixture into a 9 x 5-inch loaf pan.
Cream Cheese Filling: Mix the cream cheese, sugar and egg together. Spread this over the top of the batter, and then add the remaining batter. Bake for 50-60 minutes and golden brown.

Pickles & Chutneys

Ellen's Mother's Special Cranberries

I love this Chutney!

1 small package fresh cranberries
1 box golden raisins
3-1/2 cups sugar
1/2 cup white vinegar
1 orange—blend in food processor or blender
1 teaspoon cinnamon
1 teaspoon cloves
1 teaspoon nutmeg

Place all ingredients in a pan and cook until the cranberries pop, and the sugar had become syrupy.

Cranberry Conserve

Another of my favorites! Great for gift giving at Thanksgiving and Christmas.

4 cups fresh or frozen cranberries, halved
1 tablespoon grated orange peel
2 oranges, peeled, and sections cut away from membrane
1 cup raisins
1-1/4 cups water
1 cup chopped pecans, toasted
2-1/2 cups sugar

In a large saucepan, combine cranberries, orange peel, oranges, raisins and water. Cover and simmer over medium heat until cranberries are soft. Add pecans and sugar; stir well. Simmer uncovered 10-15 minutes, stirring often. Cool. Spoon into covered containers or sterilized glass jars. Refrigerate. Makes 3 pints.
Note: You can process the jars in a boiling water bath by following canning directions from a canning book.

Farmer's Market Pear Preserves

This is the recipe I used for the pear preserves that I sold at the Farmers Market. I had lots of gift orders for Christmas. After you make the preserves, you can use the liquid as a pear honey. Try them, it's an easy recipe.

1 pound peeled, cored pears (weigh after peeling and coring)
1-1/2 cups sugar
½ to 1 cup water
1 lemon slice

Cut pears in uniform-size pieces. Add sugar and water and cook at once. Stir while heating. Boil until tender. Then boil rapidly until syrup has thickened. Pack into hot sterilized jars and leave ½-inch head space.

Adjust the jar lids and bands. Process in a boiling water bath canner for 10 minutes, or according to canner instructions.

Remove from hot water bath and place on kitchen towels to cool. If lids do not seal, place the preserves in the refrigerator.

Super-Garlic Kosher Pickles

I've made these many times. I don't have a crock so I use a large stoneware bowl and it works just fine. You can transfer the pickles to a large jar and refrigerate later.

5 pounds blemish free blemish free pickling cucumbers, washed
2 large bunches of fresh dill, washed
(1 tablespoon additional dill seeds if fresh dill does not have a flower top with seeds)
2 cups white vinegar
1 tablespoon pickling spice
1 tablespoon dill seeds
24 cloves garlic, crushed
1/3 cup kosher salt

Place cucumbers, dill and dill weed in a large ceramic bowl or crock. In a large kettle bring the remaining ingredients to a boil. Take off the heat and let the mixture cool to lukewarm, and then pour over the cucumbers. Let the pickles stand at room temperature for 24 hours. Cover and refrigerate at least 3 days before serving. The pickles will keep covered in the refrigerator for 3-4 weeks. Makes 10-12 large pickles.
Note: When I am working with vegetables or herbs that grow on or near dirt, I wash them with a couple of drops of chlorine in the water. Then I rinse well.

Ronnie's Restaurant Kosher Style Pickles

Ronnie's was a restaurant in Orlando that closed several years ago. On the table for everyone to enjoy was Cole slaw and these pickles! The food was very good there.

Fresh cucumbers, enough to fill a five gallon crock
3 gallons water
1 pound kosher salt
3 garlic cloves, coarsely chopped
4 ounces mixed pickling spices
1 bunch fresh dill
1 loaf of stale rye bread broken into chunks

Place cucumbers in the crock. Mix salt into water and pour over cucumbers. Add garlic, spices, and fresh dill on top. Add rye bread chunks. Cover crock with cheesecloth. Put a lightweight stone on top to submerge them in the brine mixture. Keep the crock at room temperature for 3 days. Cure in the refrigerator for 5 days. Pickles must be stored in the refrigerator.

Did You Know—

Herbs—½ teaspoon dried herbs are equal to 1 tablespoon fresh herbs.

Onions—Jumbo is over 1 pound, Large is ¾-1 pound, medium is ½-¾ pound, and small is below ½ pound.

That you can substitute juices for alcohol in cooking-

2 T. Orange flavored liqueur = 2 T. orange juice
2 T. Brandy or Rum = ½ teaspoon to 1 teaspoon rum or brandy extracts (add water to the extracts if you need the extra liquid)
2 T. Amaretto or Almond flavored liqueur = ¼ to ½ teaspoon of almond extract
2 T. Sherry or bourbon = 1 to 2 teaspoon vanilla extract
2 T. Kahlua, coffee liqueur or chocolate liqueur = ½ teaspoon to 1 teaspoon of chocolate extract plus ½ to 1 teaspoon instant coffee granules in 2 T. water
White wine—equal amount of white grape juice
Red wine-equal amount of red grape juice

2 Tablespoon alcohol equals 1 ounce

Products for Personal Chef Services

- At your local "Paper Store" you will find clear pie containers, cake containers, Chinese carry-out paper boxes, and aluminum containers with tops in almost any size you need, and most of them are micro-wavable. Also ask the bakery department in your local grocery for tall pie containers.

- Find plastic containers for freezing in the grocery store.

- Check out online sites as well.

There are certain items that do not freeze well such as—

- Heavy cream, milk or sour cream unless whipped or used in casserole.

- Mayonnaise, unless cooked in a casserole.

- Celery, tomatoes, cucumbers, salad greens, eggplant, zucchini, unless cooked in a casserole.

- Raw vegetables must be blanched first.

- Cooked egg whites, unless chopped and in a casserole.

- Uncooked egg whites in an icing.

Storing & Reheating—

- Refrigerate or freeze food as soon as possible after cooking. Refrigerator thermometer should stay at 33 to 40 degrees at all times. The temperature should be at the lowest when your refrigerator is packed full of food. The freezer should be below 0.

- For several items to be chilled, quick chill in ice water if necessary so that you don't bring down the temperature of your refrigerator or freezer and ruin the food already in your fridge. Then refrigerate immediately. You may also want to place items in shallow containers so the food will chill faster in the refrigerator.

- DO NOT thaw frozen food on your countertop. Place it in the refrigerator overnight for cooking the next day, or defrost in the micro-wave, and cook right away. This method of thawing helps to preserve the texture of the food, and to keep it safe from bacteria.

- Reheat food to an internal temperature of 170 degrees. The food should be hot and bubbly.

- Do not refreeze food that has been frozen and re-heated.

- You can refreeze food that was frozen raw, and then cooked. Example: Raw ground beef cooked can be refrozen. But, once cooked, frozen and thawed, it can't be re-frozen.

Useful Items—

- Refrigerator thermometer

- Freezer thermometer

- Instant read food thermometer

- Re-usable food containers that go from freezer to oven

978-0-595-42739-0
0-595-42739-1

Printed in the United States
98747LV00003B/67/A